The Groom Wore WHITE Socks

Stories by **Charles Parish**
as written by **Logan Seth Ramirez**

Illustrated by Lindsay Irvin

The Groom Wore White Socks
White Socks Books, LLC

Copyright © 2016 by Logan Ramirez & Charles Parish

First Edition

ISBN 978-0-9982872-0-1 Hdk

Book illustration by Lindsay Irvin

Printed in the United States of America
at OneTouchPoint-Southwest in Austin, Texas

WHAT READERS HAVE SAID . . .

You will enjoy Charles Parish's truly "happy" read. Each story shows his sensitive connectivity with humanity under stress, and each memory ends with a philosophical "study lesson."

—Tom Frost, Frost National Bank, Senior Chairman of the Board

The Groom Wore White Socks is a book we were waiting to have in our hands! The combination of Charles Parish/Logan Ramirez/Lindsay Irvin is a tour de force. I have learned through nearly 60 years of "doing" marriages that the stories wedding services generate are the laughter and tears of humanity, and I congratulate our "combo" for bringing us tales of delight in written form.

—The Rev. Raymond Judd, Trinity University Chaplain Emeritus

Charles Parish has fortunately preserved the often hilarious moments that jar the life of a professional photographer but are rarely recorded. He seems to have seen it all, from a pack of favorite golden retrievers loping down the aisle to a sprinkler system suddenly dousing those at an outdoor wedding. Moreover, to avoid one sort of crisis, he had the foresight to register to perform weddings when the preacher didn't show up. A collection of truly entertaining and cautionary tales.

—Lewis Fisher, Founder, Maverick Publishing Company,

It is a pleasure and privilege when asked to express an opinion about someone's work ethic and working ability—especially when that person is Charles Parish, whom I have worked with for the 52 years he has been in business as a professional photographer.

Weddings are the most important day in the lives of young ladies, and pictures presented to them for precious memories of the special occasion should be taken by a professional like Charles.

I must pay tribute to Charles who as a professional here describes for all of us the many parts of life that "just happen." These tales also show us how composed and sensible he was with these James Bond moments in his tuxedo.

—Rosemary Kowalski, The RK Group

Considering how long I've known Charles, I'm just glad I wasn't mentioned in his book! He has photographed three generations of my family—from weddings to children to parties. Charles is always professional, thoughtful, and conscientious. It has been a pleasure being the happy beneficiary of his talents and skills.

—Lamar Smith, Texas Congressman

Table of Contents

FOREWORD

As with many good and wondrous things that unfold in the church, I have the honor of writing this because I happened to be there when the guy Charles came looking for wasn't. But being second choice isn't always bad: Charles certainly won't expect as much from me as he would his first choice, and he surely won't expect me to rave about his talents as a photographer (which are amazing) or his character (which is admirable, especially in one who is such a character). He likes to tease and give me a hard time, so he deserves no less.

A book of funny wedding stories should be very popular. It's likely that many people will suspect somebody got hold of their story and put it in here. Most clergy have a pocketful of these things. Weddings—like marriages—are prone to the darndest things: beauty and laughter intermingle with chaos and tears. Plans are exactingly made, and then life happens.

Emotions and helpful aunts run rampant, and clergy—like wedding photographers—learn to expect the unexpected. We discover that perfection is as unreasonable a goal for a wedding as it is for a marriage. A wedding well done provides an enduring pattern and picture for the marriage, maybe especially when a couple of things go wrong.

Many wedding stories that clergy tell end with something like, "And that's the day I learned never again to allow such-and-such in a wedding." Photographers certainly have those kinds of stories. Indeed, some of my favorite wedding stories involve wedding photographers (it wasn't all funny at the time), and it worries me that Charles may have some stories of his own that involve clergy doing and saying amusing (or disastrous) things.

I know some clergy who avoid officiating at weddings whenever possible. There can be lots of stress and drama, and lots of people with strong opinions. "I'd rather do a funeral," one told me. "There's no rehearsal, and nobody ever argues with me." I imagine there are fine professional photographers who feel the same way.

I'm glad to say Charles Parish isn't one of them. He is an artist and a craftsman with a sharp eye for beauty and light and the right moment, and the evidence of that can be found in wedding portraits and albums stretching back decades. He is really, really good, and he has helped many young photographers become really good, too. So many of his photos radiate joy, I think, because he is a joyful man who delights in his art and, more importantly, delights in the people he photographs and in the life unfolding before him.

Charles has been doing this for more than 50 years—a remarkable career during which he has recorded some of the most significant moments in people's lives with the click of a shutter. I can't tell that his passion for excellence or his love for his craft has diminished one bit over the years. He enjoys going to work, day after day.

I'm confident you'll have fun reading these stories. Behind the stories is Charles, who has told countless stories with his pictures and now uses actual words. The stories reveal that, while he takes his work very seriously, he doesn't take himself so seriously. He likes a good laugh (in fact, he has a good laugh), and it's appropriate that, after all these years of inviting us to be drawn into the beauty and rich humanity of his photography, he now shares with us the fun and laughter.

—The Rt. Rev. David Reed, Bishop Coadjutor of the Diocese of West Texas

Introduction

When Charles asked if I would consider writing *The Groom Wore White Socks* I immediately turned him down. Any time available between my two other full-time jobs, board involvement, volunteer soccer coaching, university affinity groups and playing music was tied up in trying to love my overly considerate wife expecting baby #4, caring for babies #1–#3, and another book. That is, I said "No" not because the idea wasn't interesting but because, more simply, I did not want to fit it in my schedule.

But like so many of the wedding stories in this collection, the way we plan things often isn't how they actually go. And thank God for that! After several days I found myself still thinking about the opportunity. After several conversations with my wife, we decided to make it work. I am so very grateful that we did.

I do not know any other relatively young men (or women for that matter) who have an opportunity to listen to someone like Charles, someone with more experiences in one lifetime than many would have in several. But for those of us fortunate enough to listen, we are forever changed—not because the stories reveal humanity in a way unknown to us, but because the story teller himself is the real story. Getting to know Charles and Betty over the last year has been a great honor, and the stories we worked through to create this collection has shaped the way I see the world which does not simply impact my life, but all of the lives with which I am involved. For opening my eyes, Charles, "Thank you."

As for the book, on the surface each story stands alone as funny or serious, but as a collection they represent something I feel is terribly important: what it means to be human. And while that question may have various answers, a mentor and friend of mine (paraphrasing Jean Vanier's book *Becoming Human*) taught me that humanity is discovered through belonging, and I can think of no other place from which we get to experience the reality of belonging-ness more than inside the bonds of marriage.[1] In my own life I have experienced the joy of belonging in many ways, but the most impacting has been through coupling my life to Hallie. In our short 10 years of marriage, I feel like we have lived through virtually every cliché imaginable, and the personal growth we have experienced may be what life is all about. Life may actually be about something else entirely, of course, but I, like everyone in this book, am on the journey to figuring that out. Writing this book has been a huge help in the process.

My overly romantic hope for *The Groom Wore White Socks* is that through these stories someone will discover a foothold in humility and step into it, uncertain of what is at the top of the climb but confident their foot is firmly planted in the right next step to get there.

My less fluffy hope is simply that readers will laugh.

Charles, thank you for the wonderful stories and friendship. Kathleen (Davis Niendorff), thank you for the excellent editing, advice (and the homemade scones). Lindsay (Irvin), thank you for the wonderful artwork, encouragement, and conversation. Hallie (my wife), thank you for creating space for me to write—literally in the form of a desk and taking the kids on adventures outside the house so I could write.

Lastly, I'm proud to say that only one of the stories in this book reminded me of my own wedding. I will not, however, say which one.

---

[1] http://www.jean-vanier.org/en/his_message/jean_vanier_on_becoming_human/to_be_fully_human

PREPARATIONS

THE WORLD'S FAVORITE PASTIME

Chewing gum is literally the world's most common habit. It is a timeless tradition that dates back over 9,000 years to when cavemen teenagers compacted birch resin and chomped away.[1] It is manufactured in 30 different countries by more than 100 companies in one-can-only-imagine how many flavors. Something about chewing gum has offered its partakers relaxation and comfort for as long as we have observable history, which should help explain why more than 100,000 tons of the stuff is consumed every single year. If

---

[1] http://www.chewinggumfacts.com/chewing-gum/about-chewing-gum/

baseball's popularity is what made it America's favorite pastime, then there is a statistical argument one can make that "gum chewing" is the favorite pastime of the world.

One hundred thousand tons per year comes out to 273 tons per day. To frame that differently, think about the last time you went to the zoo and saw a big, wrinkly, thick skinned, gray elephant. If you're lucky, maybe he or she is doing something cool and exciting like eating peanuts. Now imagine 91 of those magnificent creatures made of perfectly pink bubble gum walking in and out of the zoo every...single...day.[2]

That is a whole lot of gum.

Accumulating that kind of mass means every person in the world (of gum-chewing age, of course) must consume 280 sticks per year or, to put it another way, three out of every four days we're practicing the world's favorite pastime.

Given those facts—that gum chewing is relaxing, been around more or less as long as humans have, and 75% of the time we're chomping away on it—I suppose what is really surprising when I pointed out to the bride (moments before walking down the aisle) that she was chewing gum was not the embarrassed, "Oh shit!" response or that she ejected the massive salivated bubbalicious ball directly into my unexpecting hand, but that it hadn't happened sooner.

STORY LESSON: Make sure folks are done chewing gum before they leave the dressing room and consider making a public announcement (or likely several) to the entire wedding party. I have seen bridal parties chomping away up front so many times it is embarrassing. Oh yeah, and keep a disposable moist towelette in your pocket. There are lots of reasons that will come in handy.

---

[2] Assuming the elephant you are recalling is an African elephant. Asian elephants are more or less 2x as big so if you happen to be imagining an Asian one, then it'd be 45 and a half. That half weirds me out so I just imagine an African one.

DRESS DELIVERY

Having dresses delivered the day of the wedding may seem like a risky proposition but, from my experience, it is safer than picking them up yourself. Yes, the process is wholly out of your control and a lot of things could go wrong (like traffic or vehicle trouble), but the majority of the same problems exist if you do it yourself. In fact, I'd argue that picking up your dresses days in advance is riskier and markedly more stressful because it is one more thing you have to ensure doesn't get lost or stolen or spilled on. At least when you outsource delivery, you are paying for a certain amount of professionalism in the hopes that they know what they are doing.

That said, either way you go Murphy will invariably make his way into the world of clothing and some bride or bridesmaid or combination thereof is going to be in the dressing room moments before the ceremony with a ruined or possibly absent dress and will quite likely be crying uncontrollably as a result. Should you find yourself in this unfortunate situation, in the midst of a room full of women who cannot contain their perfectly natural emotional response to an obviously bad situation, for the love of everything pink and perfect, do not inform them that, "Crying won't do you any good!" The crying is helping a good deal more than you realize. Someone will come through, the wedding will proceed, and everyone will be reminded that people and relationships always matter substantially more than clothing.

It's just another reason dress delivery isn't that risky a proposition. Telling a woman who is emotionally invested to stop crying, on the other hand, is about as risky as it gets!

STORY LESSON: Having empathy matters when playing an instrumental role in a social gathering. Try to remember that things rarely go as planned, and people's reactions to unpredictable situations are out of your control. And that's a good thing!

The Groom Wore White Socks

For better or for worse, wedding culture sure has changed over the years. Folks marry later in life with the brides tending to be older than the groom (not to mention smarter). Prenuptials are par for the course. And best of luck finding a virgin. Tattoos are not only visible but often featured, and traditional wedding rules, along with traditional wedding locations, have all gone out the window.

While certainly still considered a formal event, the time-honored tradition of the wedding ceremony has undergone dramatic changes over the last 50 years and there is little reason to think it's done changing. I imagine during the next 50 we will establish new seemingly beneficial standards in things like vow terms and sexual orientation and gluten-free desserts as we strive for the better and not for the worse. But one thing I hope we never compromise on is its being okay for the groom to wear white socks. I just can't see how that is going to be better for anyone.

STORY LESSON: There are few, if any, things more precious than the union of a couple in a wedding ceremony, but not everyone understands or respects that. That's ok. Do your best to honor the tradition with reverence and accept those who may not meet your expectations. (I'm not saying it's easy....)

THE MEN WERE GONE

I take the pictures of the men first because they have the bulk of game day responsibilities. Then, after finishing the pictures of the women, I typically circle back to see how the men are getting along. Now, it's not entirely uncommon to find the room empty when I return, but what I walked into one particular wedding day didn't feel empty: it felt abandoned. Sure enough, after the sexton verified he saw a group of entertainers take off in their cars, I informed the father of the bride that the groom was gone.

Of course, today one might simply call the groom on his cell phone and ask what the hell was going on (or, more tersely, text him a quizzical emoticon), but this was before all that existed. The best we could do then was wait and see if he came back.

He didn't.

People came, music played, the bride and her maidens waited as patiently as one can reasonably expect. Eventually, the father of the bride walked down the aisle and announced the disappointing surprise, "There would be no wedding today...but," he continued, "there will still be a party."

Turns out, many folks didn't think the marriage was a good idea to begin with; even the few folks who came on the groom's side seemed relieved. It certainly didn't happen without tears and anger and all kinds of other emotions one can only hope never to experience, but by the end of what should have been a terrible day, sweet smiles and lovely laughter trickled over all who came, even the bride.

While this is not the kind of surprise anyone would wish for, it goes to show that even surprises themselves can be surprising.

STORY LESSON: While Hollywood may make you think weddings are abandoned all the time, I've only witnessed three (out of more than 4,000). Some of the best steps a couple can take are to have even the mildest of pre-marital counseling and be willing to listen to honest friends and family.

18

Dressmaker Forgot to Make Dresses

"Oh, I just heard the great news on your daughter's engagement, Cindy![3] Congratulations!" said the friend. "Listen, I want to help. Let me make the bridesmaid dresses."

"Oh wow! Thank you, Jillian![4] And THANK YOU! John and I were just talking about the cost of this entire thing, and I know how talented a seamstress you are, and that would be such a blessing.[5] Let me know how much the material is and, at least, let us pay for that."

"No, no, no. It's my gift to y'all. "

"Again, thank you!"

Given the title of this chapter, it may be obvious how this conversation ended in real life. Despite numerous check-ins leading up to the event, three days before the wedding Cindy informed Jillian that the project was more difficult than she realized, and the dresses would not be done in time. It doesn't matter the reasons, that kind of news always leads

---

[3] Not her real name.
[4] Not her real name, either. The last name, though—the one I didn't actually write—that's real.
[5] While not his real name, if you change three letters out and add two more, it rhymes with it.

to two places—somewhere to get last-minute dresses and somewhere far away from that friend. While Cindy not only paid triple for dresses that didn't fit well or match the color palate as closely as they should have, she paid more in a severed friendship.

STORY LESSON:: Weddings can be expensive. Specifically, in America, we're talking an average of $31,000 (and growing) expensive![6] A common way to combat that rising cost is to leverage the generosity of friends and family and their willingness to donate their time and money towards the big occasion. From my experience, this works remarkably well with things like setup and tear down, music, DJ-ing, singers, floral arrangement, party planning, bubbles for blowing, etc. When it comes to bridesmaid dresses, however, unless your Cindy is offering either a flat-out greenback donation or owns a manufacturing store, I strongly suggest staying away from letting someone make them.

---

[6] http://www.huffingtonpost.com/2015/03/13/average-cost-of-wedding-2014_n_6864860.html

Is this Trinity?

The couple entered, informed the usher they were friends of the bride, were escorted in, and sat down on the left. They smiled and shook hands with folks around them, greatly enjoying the marvelous string quartet while admiring the thoroughly impressive floral arrangements. The vibrant colors, the aromatic flowers, the acoustically perfect music, everything was absolutely beautiful—better, in fact, than they expected.

They'd never met the groom, but as he walked in they both agreed he was exceedingly handsome—exceedingly older than they expected, too. In his 50's maybe? This couple had an eight-year gap between them, so who were they to judge a 15- or 20-year spread. To each his/her own. As long as they loved each other and if the gorgeous wedding ceremony was any reflection of that love, then clearly things were going well.

Indeed, everything about this moment felt right. Except, of course, the realization a few moments later that they were at the wrong wedding.

As the bride made her way past the couple the woman casually whispered to her fellow, "That's not my friend."

"What?!" he whispered back, almost unable to control his volume.

"The bride. That's not my friend. I don't know who she is."

The man took out the invitation from his pocket and verified the time—7PM at Trinity Church. He checked is watch. 7PM. Because he had driven he also knew they were definitely at the church at Trinity.

And then it dawned on both of them: they were at the church at Trinity. Not at Trinity Church! They had gone to the church on the campus of Trinity University, not the chapel at Trinity Church two blocks west.

"Should we leave?" he asked, just as everyone bowed their heads for the invocation.

"Of course we should," she began, bowing her head, too, "but then again, this wedding is pretty nice."

So they did what any reasonable couple might do in that situation.

They stayed.

It really was a lovely ceremony.

STORY LESSON: I cannot count the number of times I've informed someone they were at First Baptist and not First Presbyterian, or Trinity Baptist not Trinity Church, or Christ Episcopal and not the Church of Christ. I don't know why so many establishments share such similar names in close proximity, but about half the time someone seems to end up at the wrong place, which is particularly problematic when it's the florist or the minister! Be sure to clarify the location as best you can or just get married at The Flippin Church of God in Arkansas[7]—nobody is going to mess that one up.

---

[7] Yes. It's real. http://www.flippincog.org/

FLOWERS DELIVERED

I have always had an appreciation for the floral arrangements at social gatherings, especially ones that feature peonies[8] or tulips. The tradition dates back to thousands of years when Egyptians would feature specific varieties to represent specific traditions.[9]

---

[8] At least ever since a southern belle friend of mine informed me the pronunciation was markedly similar to the way "Us Southerners pronounce panties."

[9] https://en.wikipedia.org/wiki/History_of_flower_arrangement

Roses represent love while jasmine exudes elegance and grace. Carnations shout pride and beauty while sunflowers beckon purity. Snapdragons promote graciousness and strength while lilacs sends a message of youthful innocence and confidence.

Each flower brings its own tradition and the culmination of all those traditions over all generations throughout all cultures over all time in a real sense grounds the ceremony into the whole of human history. When looked at from that angle, flowers can be a humbling reminder of who we are, where we've come from, and even offer a small glimpse of where we're going.

Unless, of course, the flowers are delivered to another church. When that happens, we aren't reminded of a single thing.

STORY LESSON: Mistakes happen and, while unfortunate, social ceremonies are not exempt. Try to remember the people around you daily matter so much more than the things that will be around you that one single day.

Everything was Stolen

Not all social gathering stories are pleasant. Just about every event I've done has had some element of undesirable drama, but perhaps the worst is when something gets stolen. I am not talking about something going missing, like a present, but rather I mean undeniable theft—such as all of the presents or the card box (containing cards with money usually) disappearing or all of the rented tuxedos and shoes walking away. I am talking about the type of violation where an unwelcome intruder leaves an indescribably dark blemish on what could have been, should have been a bright day.

I remember one wedding planner's strategy focused so heavily on reducing stress during the event that they staged as much as possible at the chapel the night before. Dresses in the bridesmaid room pressed and hung with care, tuxedos and shoes separated far enough to allow for individual changing areas, flowers filling the entire chapel all night long with aromatic splendor, and the wedding programs meticulously laid out in the foyer. The idea makes perfect sense. By streamlining the work the night before, everyone involved can enjoy the wedding day without any of the inevitable interruptions of pre-event task management.

Sadly, the idea also introduces terrible risk. Should someone break into the chapel the night before, they'd have access to everything. They'd be able to singlehandedly destroy months of planning in about 30 minutes. Instead of reducing stress on the wedding day, the plan effectively introduced more than anyone could reasonably handle. It's the kind of thing that does not just blemish the day but virtually destroys it.

STORY LESSON: While nobody really wants to arrive early and set up the ceremony, it's the only way to reduce this risk. Leaving all of the key elements centralized in an unguarded building for the sake of reducing what ends up actually only being minutes of set-up time isn't worth it. Plus, from my experience, folks in the wedding party like being involved, enjoy setting up, and don't mind carrying in their clothes. Accept the help and let them love you with their service.

WHERE'S THE PREACHER?

Nobody said anything to the bride or groom. Why would they? The traveling justice of the peace still had a healthy 30 minutes to arrive, and it wasn't uncommon for him to show up "at the last minute" anyway. At least, that's what the venue, the party responsible for providing the professional "legal binder," told the family. They still had time. No good reason to worry them.

Still, even knowing he blatantly disregarded timeliness did little to ease the tension slowly drifting across the room. Person by person, the murmurs permeated, and it was only a matter of time before the whispers seeped into the dressing rooms. With each passing minute, the question loomed louder, and everyone knew that sooner rather than later they would have to answer, "What were they going to do if the preacher didn't show?!"

What else? Ask the photographer to marry them, of course! It just so happens I was already registered in this particular county as a legal officiant.

With 10 minutes to go, my business partner pulled up a standard set of wedding vows on her iPad and walked up to the parents letting them know that, should they desire, I could legally officiate. Without hesitation, they gratefully agreed. The wedding proceeded; I took pictures during the ceremony; Jenna Beth read the vows;[10] and after the ceremony I signed the certificate.

Looking back on it, I'm not sure the bride and groom even realized it wasn't planned that way! Either way, like I said all along, there really was no reason to worry.

STORY LESSON: It's not exactly uncommon for ministers to show up late (or early) to a wedding. They are typically booked months in advance and, particularly in their profession, emergencies tend to disrupt schedules. While it certainly doesn't change how downright rude and disruptive the effect, it is really uncommon for them not to show up at all!

---

[10] I'm too old to read from those things. Thank God for Jenna Beth!

WE JUST NEED EIGHT MORE

It is surprisingly simple to make most floral bouquets and, for anyone involved with social event planning, it is a skill one should practice because a day will come when too few bouquets exist for the required needs. And when that day comes, someone at the wedding will lose his or her freaking mind. Yup, lose their cool over having too few flowers.

To be fair, however, the small things are the metaphorical "straw" that invariably seems to break the "camel's back," and planning for a wedding ceremony has substantially more straw than people realize. So, statistically speaking, it is quite likely going to be a seemingly small thing—like a shortage of flowers—that puts a stressed planner over the edge. Still, despite the reasonable justifiability for Mama GiGi to hand that innocent delivery person a new bottom, having too few bouquets is an easy problem to fix.

I've done it more times than I can remember and have managed to manufacture as many as eight additional bouquets from what was delivered by simply un-tying the existing ones, re-grouping them (pulling from around the church if required[11]), and tying them back together. It really is surprisingly simple. Untie, re-group, re-tie. To quote Disney Junior's Agent Oso, all it takes is "three special steps."

If, however, you're still concerned about doing it, there is these days always the Internet. There's always YouTube. You'll quite likely find several "How To Put Together a Bouquet" videos in between the endless supply of "Funny Cat" ones. And while you're there, might as well search for a few "Folks Losing Their Freaking Mind" videos to remind you of what you're helping to prevent happening.

---

[11] Most of the time the additional flowers used were from the wedding itself; however, admittedly, yes, I did technically steal from a church one time.

STORY LESSON: Its obviously better if the florist delivers eight bouquets when you only need six; however, should you need to create another, perhaps even because of a last-minute bridesmaid addition (or, perhaps, an unruly and envious four-year-old flower girl), it really isn't that difficult to create more of them. Take your time and use your naturally creative energy to take on yet another unplanned role. It's just another day at the office for a wedding photographer.

FORMER WIFE SHOT BY GROOM

I've had the good fortune and the honor of being a part of thousands of weddings. You name it; I've seen them all: themed, classic, modern, extravagant, overly extravagant, modest, overly modest, simple, obscure, celebrity, popular, unpopular, sexually ambiguous, and every ambiguity in between. I've seen the highest highs majestically painted crimson with unfettered love and I've seen the lowest lows filtered through the darkest opacity. And while the beautiful ones fill our spirits up with seemingly infinite amounts of faith, hope, and love, their tragic counterparts juxtapose the terrible, and possibly immutable, truth that humanity is, or at least can be, at times very broken. It might be a classic case of cold feet where the bride or groom just cannot go through with the ceremony or the unfortunate case of an untimely car crash where injury or death interrupt not just the day but multiple lives over possibly multiple lifetimes. Regardless, any and all social events are just like any everything else: vulnerable to the viral reach of the unpredictable.

The most unpredictable I have experienced, however, was the day the groom did not show because he was arrested for shooting his ex-wife's nose off! While a complete framing of the story reveals the groom's innocence, that the former wife brought the weapon to the groom's home and the firing happened in self-defense, it does not change the outcome—the wedding would be rescheduled on account of the groom's detention for shooting his ex-wife. And although there may be countless divorced men who in their own broken way applaud such a headline, the wedding day for those families and friends was ruined.

What do you do when something like that happens? More pressing for the people in the moment, what do you tell them!? I hope a script does not exist for such unexpected news, but in this case the minister simply announced there wouldn't be a wedding and then made a humble suggestion: because everyone was already dressed so nicely, perhaps they should check out the symphony.

Indeed, many did.

STORY LESSON: While this couple did get married a few weeks later, the story serves as a constant reminder of an old adage that when you marry someone, you marry all of their baggage too, including, but not limited to, their family, friends, and, former failed relationships. There is no way to know all the things you're getting and, although it's tempting to let that uncertainty deter you from moving forward, I've discovered more times than not that in the end that same uncertainty is also what quite often makes marriage so terribly exciting and unique. Even though I don't particularly recommend it, I'm also not explicitly against adding, "To the best of your knowledge, do any of your ex's own a gun and plan to use it on the parties present?" to your pre-marriage questionnaire. Your call.

THE CEREMONY

Best Bridesman Ever

While not mainstream by any means, I have witnessed a surprising number of bride's men standing proudly in line with bridesmaids over the years, and I've even taken pictures of several weddings that featured men of honor in place of the traditional maid. It always makes for wonderful conversation and I go out of my way to have it, to learn the back story behind this relatively rare moment. As one might expect, the bridesmen are typically a brother or a best friend, but one story that has particularly inspired me was a relatively new male friend who had saved the bride's life. Not from a physical danger like pulling her from a burning building but rather by pulling her out of the even more precariously emotional dark and lonely bottom of depression.

About a year before the wedding the bride hit a near suicidal state when her father died of AIDS, having hidden from his family his homosexual disposition, which led to numerous affairs and the fatal prognosis. I know that is the kind of story found in a Hollywood plot line, not real life. Nonetheless, this precious child found herself a main character in it.

As most of us could only imagine, and none of us desire to actually know, the emotional blow back of the news took many who loved him by surprise and sent this beautiful would-be bride into a state from which nobody thought she could recover. That is, until she met the bridesman. This new friend had gone through his own emotional roller coaster as he navigated the revelation of his own homosexual nature and understood what it felt like being down in a metaphorically deep hole and that when there, when you are down in the pitch-black bottom, you do not need someone to tell you how to get out, but rather, to paraphrase research professor Brene Brown in her TED talk on the difference between sympathy and empathy, what you need is, "someone to climb down the ladder and say they know what it feels like and that you're not alone."[12] While well intentioned, you do not need someone to offer you a sandwich or string together

---

[12] http://brenebrown.com/videos/

a set of at-least-you-have-such-and-such affirmations but rather someone to be present, to listen, and to hold you. To be there so you are not alone.

And that was exactly what he helped her see—that she wasn't. She wasn't alone then, and she certainly wasn't alone on her wedding day, and a big reason was because this noble young man used his own painful life experiences to extend the kind of empathy she needed, to give a friend the kind of love that matters.

I've had the honor of being a part of so many special events, but that moment, that bride, that young man, and that story managed not just to change the course of that wedding but the course of my own life as well.

Plus, as stereotypical as it is, to this day I have never seen a better-dressed attendant! He apparently not only knew how to put hearts together but also how to color coordinate a vintage waistcoat with the bridesmaids' dresses.

STORY LESSON: People matter. I cannot stress that enough. So many folks get caught up in the nuances of the day's events, fretting over failed flower arrangements or undercooked food, but inside and around all of the social event are real people with real stories filled with their own failures and "undercooking," all of which have uniquely equipped them to be human. Don't miss out on a story that might change you.

THE BEST MAN WAS BLACK

I hope you never heard the one about that wedding where nobody came because the best man was black. But I have.

It was 1954, the same year the Supreme Court[13] famously overturned the long-standing separate-but-equal tradition so pervasive throughout North America. It was a time in which, other than in baseball and the military, virtually all aspects of society had more or less one visible color palate for its patrons, and that included weddings. So the boycott wasn't exactly surprising. Still it's the kind of thing today you hope never to see, let alone be part of; it's the kind of thing we can hope that those who absented themselves look back on with regret.

And that piece of it, the part where I wonder how society could ever have been so obtuse, is the part I find the most frustrating about stories like these, about stories of blatant ignorance. Because while we have made significant strides the last 60 years in breaking down racial barriers, I'm not sure society by and large has noticeably moved further along in accepting others. Heck, forget about society, I am not sure I have moved any further along! And that is terribly frustrating to me near the end of my own lifetime, this indictment of humanity and the indictment of me.

It is with great pride I filter back through my portfolio and observe trending acceptance of racial integration, but woven in the same book are countless other reasons folks invented to boycott and abandon relationships. It might have been economic status or sexual orientation or skin color or the number of tattoos or a general lack of civility or an associated relationship or a maturity problem (from either or both sides) or whatever; in the end, while it is tempting to celebrate the progress we've made in racial bigotry, [14] bigotry itself persists.

---

[13] *Brown vs The Board of Education*
[14] And it is absolutely worth celebrating

So although you may not have heard about the day nobody showed because the best man was black, odds are good that if you take the time to look around, you'll have heard of something similar.

STORY LESSON: I've written it several times already, but people matter. That simple guideline has carried me a long way in life, but it alone hasn't managed to save me from classic foot-in-mouth syndrome. Granted, some social events go better when certain folks don't show up, but when they don't show up because of an unfairly grounded bias, it can put a big dent in the day. Theologian and professor Reinhold Niebuhr may have said it best in his relatively famous serenity prayer, "God grant me the serenity to accept the things I cannot change, the courage to change the things I can, and the wisdom to know the difference." I am not sure we can rightly have hope to change the world but, with even an ounce of humility, we can have a good deal of hope in changing ourselves.

DOUBLE WEDDINGS

While sharing a wedding reduces some costs, it introduces a good deal of logistical complexity, especially for twins. One example might be wedding gifts. While not as frustrating for twin brides, it can be particularly frustrating for blood-related grooms who share a last name. Unless you want to spend hours sorting gifts, extra care must be taken at the reception to separate them correctly. Another obvious example is head count. While slightly less of a problem for sisters or brothers who share an invite list, doubling the head count requires doubling the capacity for a venue, which may even mean doubling the price— and good-bye cost savings. Another consideration is the additional burden it places on the officiant to get all the names right. That poor man or woman has the task of navigating the names of not just two people but four on one of the most important days of their lives. It's an easy enough mistake when there is only one couple, but when there are two couples and two of the people are identical twins, you can just bank on some name mistakes. In fact, I would venture to say while every wedding is, of course, vulnerable to the embarrassing name slip, a wedding with two separate couples where the set of brides or grooms actually look the same is guaranteed to have one. I'll make that bet every time.

In one particular twin wedding, however, the priest did something to prevent the mistake that would have cost my bet: he placed two pieces of masking tape on the inside front edge of the pulpit with the respective couples names on either side. This way every time his eyes traveled from the marrying party down to his hand-held material and back up again, he could glance at the well-placed nametag and have the right person in mind as he addressed them! Brilliant!

Or, at least, it would have been had the groomsmen not taken notice during rehearsal and swapped the tape strips. Through the entire wedding ceremony this poor fellow mistakenly spoke with confidence the wrong name of each bride and groom. Several times they made subtle attempts to correct him, but either he was so confident in his method or they were just too concerned with disrupting the ceremony that the message never got through.

In that particular case, should the names be tampered with by self-proclaimed co-medians who think themselves exceedingly funnier than they actually are, the odds of a name slip increases exponentially. And it's just another reason I'd place the original bet.

STORY LESSON: Unless the bride and groom know the minister well, it really is a challenge for the marrying pastor to get the names right. In the end, should it happen, do your best to grant them the kind of grace you'd want or follow the golden rule and treat them as you'd want to be treated—with an ounce of understanding and a whole mess of forgiveness.

42 Bridesmaids

Speaking of logistical issues, one of the most challenging I've observed is when a bride or groom invites an entire platoon[15] (or greater!) to stand up for them. Aside from the extended length of time it takes to bring them down the aisle, having enough space for them to stand up front is always a game of Tetris[16] during rehearsal, let alone the exercise of repeating it during the actual ceremony. In the end, the formation usually ends up in stacked rows so they themselves look like a human bouquet and, while it's actually quite beautiful, if the bridal party is not dressed well and/or placed properly, it can end up an unexpected distraction.

In the case of one small-town Texas wedding, the bride had 42 maidens[17] and the distraction was partly attributable to venue (the church was not large enough to allow for 42 folks to stand anywhere near comfortably) but primarily a result of the economic law of supply and demand: there wasn't enough fabric for that many outfits in this small town. Either too proud to turn down the job or not creative enough to adopt a coordinated color palate or whatever, the seamstress used varying material with subsequently varying shades of the desired red. While up close a merlot chiffon might look good against a rose georgette which might look fine next to a blush satin, when you group the mix-and-match lot together in full-size fashion under traditional vintage chapel lighting, the result is regrettable.

Even four-time Tetris champion of the world, Jonas Neubauer, couldn't work with those pieces.

STORY LESSON: If you are going to have a big bridal party, have fun with it. You are already breaking traditional rules of ceremony, so take a few more steps and ensure the outfits work en masse or just let them be really intentionally non-matching. Any way you go, know the large number of people already does enough on its own to take attention away from what should be the focus of the event—the bride (and to a much lesser degree, the groom)—so don't give it any more power than it already has.

---

[15] I do not mean a literal platoon in the military sense, but rather in quantity. A "platoon" is between 15-30 people.
[16] A classic Nintendo game of fitting pieces together.
[17] For the record, there were not 42 groomsmen.

RIGHT DAY. WRONG TIME!

Other than the bride and groom, the person who officiates at the ceremony, the person actually licensed by the local county to legalize the union, plays the next most central role in the success of the day. Ideally, the person would have some real experience under his or her belt, enjoy public speaking and actually like people, but all of those qualities fall squarely into the nice-to-have bucket—I wouldn't classify them as "mission critical." The only absolutely mandatory tasks for the officiant are (a) showing up and (b) signing the marriage certificate. If those do not happen, the day is for all intents and purposes ruined.

Another issue for everyone involved in the ceremony related to showing up, is showing up on time. And while I'd like to say that characteristic is mission critical, the reality is someone in almost every event arrives late for some forgivable reason, and the event manages to proceed just fine. Obviously the gravity of that delay falls more heavily when it's a role player, but the reason is almost always traffic or an unexpected illness or a random accident—a life interruption to which we can relate and, more importantly, cannot control. It's easier to forgive and forget those than when the delay is because the person simply wrote down the wrong start time.

Like the minister who casually strolled into the church late to be greeted by angry parents and a room full of well-dressed and antsy guests because he wrote down 11AM install of 10AM.[18] Those types of tardy reasons are far more difficult to forgive. But even then, when you think about that example a little further, you actually find yourselves grateful he made a practice of arriving early or didn't accidentally write down 10PM or else he might have missed the whole thing!

Still, frustration and forgiveness and inevitability and honest mistakes aside, when someone like the minister shows up late to an event it always ushers in a gloomy cloud that everyone hopes the sunshiny moments ahead will eradicate.

Even if I end up not tossing timeliness on to the "mission critical" stack, it's still pretty damn important.

STORY LESSON: Personally follow up with the key players for the day. It's typically a small list. The bride and groom won't have the wrong time written down, but it's not out of the question that the well-intentioned flower delivery people or the pastor wrote the wrong time—or worse, the wrong day. Minimize the stress by making a few phone call reminders the week of the event.

---

[18] Antsy may be a bit gracious.

THE BEST MAN REALLY DID FORGET THE RING

I've participated in my fair share of awkward moments, but the time the best man forgot the ring at his house and the groom told him to go back and get it *during the wedding ceremony* sits on top. How the best man managed to get all the way until the minister asked for the rings before he realized the gaffe remains outside the bounds of my finite mind, yet there he was in total panic mode searching every pocket with terror and embarrassment on his face which everyone naturally mistook for humor. Works every time for break-up laughter, right up until it's no longer funny, right up until the dreadful realization that "Holy smokes, the best man really **did** forget the ring" finishes marching its non-humorous self through the minds of everyone in the room, settling painfully in the disbelieving minds of the honored couple.

"Bro, seriously, you don't have it?" quizzed the groom, avoiding eye contact with his bride-to-be.

"Seriously. No, I don't. It's at my house."

"Well, go get it!"

The best man lived near the church, so other than perhaps proceeding with a pretend ring, the commute decision felt like the right call. The minister did his best to temper the awkward edge by asking the musicians to play and after the first song the wedding party sat down in their places while everyone uneasily waited. In the end, the whole ordeal only took about fifteen minutes, but did it feel like forever!

I've thought about that wedding a good deal over the years and, like I said, to this day I still cannot imagine how that young man managed to forget such an important thing. To this day, too, I also cannot imagine ever seeing anyone sprint out of a church any faster!

STORY LESSON: Make a checklist for each key person involved with the event, and make sure they bring them to the ceremony for your review. In today's technology heavy world, there are tons of collaborative options which integrate with smart phones and the like,[19] but don't rule out good old-fashioned paper and pen. The point is to put something in place to ensure all of the really important things get done so, at the very least, your worst fears don't come true.

---

[19] My personal favorites are Asana (http://asana.com) and Trello (http://trello.com).

Babies Don't Wait

"I need to sit down for a bit," the pregnant bride methodically stated during the pre-ceremony pictures, breathing deeply and placing her hands around her tightening belly. Still a couple of weeks from the official due date, the stress of the day coupled with a tighter-than-expected dress were visibly exacting a toll. Taking no chances, I quickly assisted her down the altar steps only to escort her back to the dressing room moments later where several of the bridesmaids helped her get comfortable. Although in visible discomfort, she didn't seem overly concerned so we continued with pictures, and I walked the maidens to the altar for their turn in front of the camera. Anxiety wafted over the party, but eventually the tension was eased with a running joke about walking back to the dressing room to find a baby, which of course would not have been funny at all if it actually happened. Fortunately, when we returned, baby was still happily absent from the festivities, but the bride had managed to remove her wedding dress and was wearing instead what I've come to learn that delivery nurses refer to as "The Happy Face."[20]

---

[20] The painful face expressed during labor… which means a baby is on the way! Happy!

Within minutes the groom joined her, followed immediately by the parents, who quickly encased the couple and began several rounds of disconcerting conversation. Eventually, the father of the bride, the baby's maternal grandfather, emerged from the huddle and somewhat disappointedly announced, "Well, looks like we're not having a wedding today."

To which the bride, now visibly energized and standing up added, "But no worries. We are going to have a baby, instead!"

All of the parents began laughing, including Disappointed Grandpa. While there may have been quite a few frustrating reasons to cancel, there was one exceptionally good reason to celebrate.

STORY LESSON: While the colloquial shotgun wedding is rarely (never, from my experience) actually rooted in coercion, the baby usually ends up being the star of the day anyway. The days of embarrassment seem to be over and, while it may or may not be an ideal situation, it is a situation worth celebrating nonetheless. Celebrate every wedding, every life, every time.

THREE FATHERS OF THE BRIDE

I have participated in countless weddings where no father gave away the bride, but I have only been a part of one where three did!

The bride's mother divorced a few weeks after delivery, and her second husband loved the mother and daughter for several years before that marriage was mutually dissolved, and a third paternal influence arrived just in time to battle the teenage years and beyond. On paper that might seem like a recipe for disaster or, at the very least, some ingredients for visible dysfunction, but by the grace of God all three male role models stood as strong, positive life influences for her, and so she wanted all three to be involved in the wedding ceremony.

Considering how easily (not to mention how often) jealously and bitterness and all kinds of other emotions interfere with ex-anythings, to witness a mutually shared love that transcended those borders was truly one of the more precious moments I've experienced. The old adage that "A father is a girl's first love" has been affirmed so often in my observation that during the whole ceremony I kept thinking how lucky this girl must feel to have these three men in her life, teaching her what it means to be valued and loved and cherished.

On the other hand the whole time I kept thinking how unlucky for the groom. It's hard enough to try and match the bar set by one father-in-law, I can't imagine trying to live up to the expectations of three!

STORY LESSON: Family dynamics are unpredictable and precious in their respective ways. It is so difficult for me to see how two divorces could pave an example of fidelity and stability, and yet here it was being displayed in practical reality. We should be careful not to let our own fortunate or unfortunate or indifferent relationship experiences filter out something valuable we can learn from someone else's.

NOBODY CARES WHAT MEN WEAR

Walk into a tuxedo rental shop today and you will find an overwhelming number of options. You'll find traditional single-breasted coats with pique lapel shirts fastened with standard studs and you'll discover ultra-modernized six-button shawl collared outerwear paired with contemporary point-tip (or possibly no-tip) shirts under who-knows-what kind of tie available in virtually every pantone color. What fascinates me, however, is not the massive spectrum from which formal men's attire has grown or the over-all movement of renting-over-owning, but how so many options have developed when, generally speaking, nobody really cares what the men wear anyway.

Now, obviously the men should wear something and preferably something nice, but beyond "something" and "nice" it really doesn't matter. Of course, don't tell some men that, but generally speaking while people attend weddings to honor the couple and celebrate life together, the bride and her magnificent dress are without question what people want to see and are ultimately what people will remember. Sure, sure, a well-dressed groom will get noticed but, for the most part, no combination of "something nice" exists for which a groom will stand out enough to matter in the day's scheme.

Take, for example, a wedding to which the groom wore flip-flops. Granted they were nicer flip-flops (not the $3.50 rubber patterned ones from Old Navy), but they were still flip-flops! Did anyone notice? Maybe. Did anyone care? Nope. Well, except for the embarrassed in-laws and me. We definitely noticed, and the in-laws definitely cared. In fact, at their request all the pictures I took that day were from the ankles up, which really just further validates that, even when looking back through timeless images when the couple's collective memory fades, the groom's outfit still won't stand out as anything beyond 'something nice' and it doesn't really matter. To be fair, because there were actually a few of us who did notice and at least one couple that did care, I should restate my opinion: other than particularly opinionated photographers and some parents, as long as the men look somewhat nice, nobody really cares what they are wearing.

STORY LESSON: Some men are just as vain as some women, if not more so! With regards to weddings, however, they shouldn't be. If there is ever a day to honor a woman, it is this one. A man should stick with simple formal wear to help keep attention where it should be anyway—on his better half.

THE DO-RE-MI-NISTER

Finding a marriage officiant who is a dynamic speaker can prove challenging, but finding one who sings his part of the ceremony is nearly impossible—at least outside Las Vegas. Not that you'd want the parts sung. Unless you specifically tell the officiant not to melodiously proclaim the vows, however, you can't really guarantee it won't happen either.

Such was the case at one unique wedding where the couple stood on the top of the altar steps facing the audience and the mic'd-up minister faced the bride and groom with his back towards the guests. Aside from the uncommon physical arrangement, the first 15 minutes of the ceremony was traditional: the procession was followed by giving away of the bride, then opening remarks leading into a beautiful first round of candle lighting and the verbal charge. Then, from what seemed like out of nowhere, the singing started. Lovely singing, but where everyone was expecting to hear the exchange of vows, we heard a dramatic baritone instead. It took awhile, but after surveying the room for the source, everyone realized the minister was singing the marriage covenant!

While I'd heard that singing releases endorphins, a hormone associated with feelings of pleasure, I had my doubts.[21] But, as I watched smiles appear on guests' faces and then heard the bride and groom sing back, "I do," I became a believer. And if you were watching my face at the time, you would have seen my endorphin-based smile give it away.

STORY LESSON: Rolling with the unexpected is a life skill few people have naturally, but it's one that can be learned. I've learned it over time, and I would say that to be successful in a services industry rolling with the unexpected is something you have to learn. Of course, it's always easier when the unexpected is a beautiful song.

---

[21] Technically, it's been proven (http://science.howstuffworks.com/life/inside-the-mind/emotions/singing-happy1.htm).

Bow Wow Wedding

Often referred to as "Man's Best Friend," dogs have long held a special place in human society. Whether starring in movies or TV shows, serving in the military, guiding the visually impaired, or simply welcoming their owner home with a giddy tail wag, something unique about the relationship between humans and canines has long captured the heart of man. Almost everyone I know, if not actually everyone I know, has at least one story of at least one dog that has impacted his or her life in at least one way for the better. So much at times, in fact, that some furry friends are invited to participate in the wedding ceremony.

My favorite featured a pack of golden retrievers the bride had rescued as puppies and loved so much that featuring them in the wedding was a requirement for the marriage. That is, if the groom wanted to marry her, then he had to agree to let her beloved pets stand up for her during the ceremony![22] Fortunately for the groom, golden retrievers are a non-territorial

---

[22] Alongside humans, too.

breed, so accepting another member into the pack was really up to him. Fortunately for the bride, the groom was also an animal lover, and so he graciously joined the family.

Not having any children to play the traditional role of flower girls or ring bearers in the ceremony, the beautiful dogs were decked out with colorful flower wreathes and had a friend to guide them down the aisle. The well-trained dogs impressively sat around the couple throughout the entire ceremony and brought a room full of laughter when they barked their own "I do." The moment brought to life words from American wildlife photographer and writer Roger Caras: "Dogs are not our whole life, but they make our lives whole."[23]

At least for that moment, they sure did.

STORY LESSON: Family tends to mean something slightly different for everyone. While traditionally the word applies to blood lineage, in a day where blended families and adoption are so common, the broader term has long applied and it has become commonplace for close friends and even animals to fall inside the ranks of those we unconditionally love. A consistent theme throughout my career has been "expect the unexpected," and there are few places that mantra rings truer than within the family circle—dogs and all.

---

[23] https://www.goodreads.com/quotes/19168-dogs-are-not-our-whole-life-but-they-make-our

NO SHIRT, NO SHOES, NO SERVICE

The third chapter of Ecclesiastes, a book in the Bible known as The Book of Wisdom, claims there is a time for everything. A time to be born and a time to die, a time to plant and time to uproot, a time to weep and a time to laugh—a time for, well, like it says, everything. I'm not one to read more into things so if a writing known as one of the greatest wisdom collections ever-assembled uses the word everything then I'd just assume it means everything. That said, I do wonder whether God and all His infinite wisdom really meant, "Yes, there is even a time in an affluent first-world country when men can forgo socks and shoes during a formal ceremony."

Don't get me wrong here. Lots of situations fall categorically into the "everything bucket" subjecting them to the same quizzical inquiry, but the ones I think of are not nearly as disconcerting as a bunch of grown men purposely choosing to bare their stinky athletic feet for everyone's displeasure. It'd be one thing if they, like Moses, had walked countless miles across a deserted land in sweat-filled sandals and removed the filthy clods out of respect for the holy ground or if the wedding took place on a beach, but I watched those young men step out of luxury sedans in shiny new oxfords, and the ceremony was in about the oldest church you could find. They simply made a last-minute decision not to wear shoes.

I don't know. Maybe God really did mean everything including barefoot formal twenty-first century weddings, but after witnessing it I couldn't help but wonder if even an omniscient God might look down every now and again and, like so many of us, want the occasional do-over.

STORY LESSON: Even the most casual wedding is still a formal occasion, and even the most casual formal attire requires shoes. You might be able to walk into a corner store and buy a gallon of milk without the store clerk calling you out, but please don't push the envelope at a social ceremony in a 150-year-old church with 500 guests.

OWN A TUXEDO AND SAVE THE WORLD

James Bond is one of the top three longest-running film franchises.[24] Debuting in 1962 with *Dr. No*, starring Sean Connery as the remarkable hero James Bond, the series has run for more than 50 years largely because it features a man who continually saves the world by doing things well outside of expected reality while exuding enviable charm and wearing a classic tuxedo. In other words, the mysteriously fantastic and ultimately rugged James Bond is also the consummate gentleman.

---

[24] The 23 *James Bond* films sit third behind 31 British comedy productions of *Carry On* and 30 *Godzilla* movies. I know, right? There are 30 *Godzilla* movies....

And while James Bond does not actually exist, the idea of chivalry he embodies is pervasive. It haunts virtually every man and resonates with virtually every woman. Over time, however, it seems that haunting is losing its ability to motivate men. While still visible, you have to squint a lot harder to find one who consistently opens doors for others, who genuinely cares for people not just the service they provide, who enjoys reading and writing, or, more simply, find one who even owns a tuxedo. In the early years of my career, all the men attending a classy wedding owned their own tuxedos. Today you rarely see it. I think that's why the James Bond series thrives: the idea he represents embodies a longing that itself longs to awaken.

I know I'll never be James Bond not just because he is fictional, but because I know how hard it is to be thoughtful, to be considerate, to be a gentlemen, and, of course, always to be exquisitely groomed. It's those small things, first, that rule me out well before the MI6 physical exam. But, for the record, I do own a tux. And while I feel light years away from resembling the hero Mr. Bonds represents, in a strange way every time I put it on I do feel one step closer.

STORY LESSON: If chivalry isn't dead it is without question rarely in evidence. I understand that times have changed, but humanity by and large hasn't: people still long for connectedness; men still thrive on respect; and women are still energized by receiving love. Obviously, owning a tuxedo doesn't make a man gentle and says very little about how he might love someone, but I would contend that a gentleman would, at the very least, consider buying one with the understanding that wearing it may well have very little to do with him and a good deal to do with loving and respecting others.

THE BRIDE'S FATHER WAS IN PRISON

There are few things more powerful emotionally than a father's walking his daughter down the aisle. As the traditional head-of-household, the father historically wielded the tangible power to unite family lines and increase domestic stability by arranging who would marry his daughters. This role made his presence on the big day tantamount to a seal of success. While today many of us may shutter at such a seemingly archaic framing, I cannot imagine dismissing the symbolism that process represents, the qualitative emotional transition of moving from being "Daddy's girl" to becoming "Mrs. Smith," as trivial. My observation from over 4,000 weddings is that if a daughter has a healthy relationship with her father (and, in some cases, even if she doesn't), having him escort her arm-in-arm down the aisle to publicly "give her away" to her soon-to-be life partner before all her family and friends is one of the most important traditions the day holds.

This immutable truth, that there is a special bond between a dad and his daughter which holds a sacred place in the wedding ceremony, is so universally understood and respected that I've seen a father granted temporary release from prison[25] so he could

---

[25] The father committed a white collar crime; he was not, for the record, a hardened murderer or the like.

walk his daughter down the aisle. It didn't come without a good deal of effort, of course, but after enough pleas to the State from the bride her father was allowed to arrive moments before the ceremony started to formally give his child away.

I hope I never forget the nearly inexpressible emotion which overwhelmed the pair when they embraced or how the immutable and enviable pride in which he held up his daughter as they seemed to glide down the aisle brought tears to nearly everyone's eyes. It was one of the most endearing moments I've ever experienced and also, as he exited immediately to go back to prison after ceremoniously giving her away, one of the most painful.

There is, of course, no way of knowing, whether that moment actually made any difference in the long-term future of that bride's marriage, but I do know with great certainty that the moment mattered a good deal to many of us fortunate enough to witness it. A lifetime of having a loving parent as symbolized by that walk is one of the most powerful moments in this life.

STORY LESSON: Being a parent is a great responsibility, arguably one of the greatest responsibilities we can take on in life. The idea of missing our child's wedding (for whatever the reason), let alone not being able to participate in the ceremony, is a painful one. The moment our lives are so intrinsically united with another, whether a spouse or a child or a lover, is the moment we should begin to weigh our decisions with an incalculably greater and immeasurably different scale. As unintuitive as it might seem at times, our lives are not our own and that is, perhaps, exactly how it is intended to be.

PHOTO OPS

THE DISAPPEARING CROSS

I have always been fascinated that people notice certain things, like pet peeves or someone acting weird with their phone, but completely miss others, like the white arrow in the FedEx logo, or when your spouse gets a new haircut … or when the traditional cross on the altar has been absent throughout the entire wedding ceremony![26]

It wasn't until the mother of the bride quizzically stated while viewing the pictures post ceremony, "I can't put my finger on it, but something just ain't right," that we noticed. After several guesses and few dismissals, we realized the central object of the altar, a 50-pound iron cross which typically sat dead center was gone!

Out of respect for the predominant belief on his side of the aisle, the Jewish groom moved the time-honored Christian symbol to a non-visible location, assuming or perhaps hoping the predominantly Christian bride's side wouldn't notice. And they almost didn't! But once they did, once his new mother-in-law pointed out something wasn't right, it set off all kinds of fireworks, to the point that someone proposed doing the ceremony over again!

Fortunately, they found common ground, and we didn't enact a do-over, but that moment opened my eyes to just how many ordinary and common things I miss out on. I was embarrassed that I failed to notice the missing cross too, but I made up for it later when I got home and told my wife Betty her new hairstyle looked lovely. It would have meant more, of course, if she had actually gotten it re-styled.

STORY LESSON: Interfaith marriages can pose challenging dynamics but typically not insurmountable ones. Some compromise will be necessarily inevitable. Hopefully, each person will also possess enough humility not to blatantly disregard the other. As for developing a set of eyes such that you notice missing objects or a new haircut, I'm still working on that!

---

[26] You're welcome, FedEx®. Sweet logo by the way!

YEA OR NEIGH

When I was told the pre-ceremony pictures were going to be on horseback, I admit I had some reservations. For folks who grew up around horses, successfully mounting a horse for pre-ceremony pictures in formal attire turns out to be a fairly trivial task.[27] Their natural understanding of general equitation and horsemanship allows them to mount a horse into an "on-the-bit" position incredibly fast, even with restrictive clothes. And it's downright inspiring when you realize they have spent years with that animal. As any serious animal owner would tell you, there is an unspoken connection between a human and his or her pet. In the case of someone who grew up working with a 2,000-pound animal described as "having been made by God from the breath of the wind, the beauty of the earth, and the soul of an angel," the connection may run even

---

[27] …and quite an impressive one to witness, I might add!

deeper.[28] Any earlier doubts I had about someone's falling off the horse or getting kicked in the head quickly disappeared when I watched the bride and groom display an obvious and inexplicably deep connection with the horses.

My doubts, however, returned abruptly when the rest of the wedding party arrived. Their interactions with the majestic beasts were quite different and displayed a connection more closely allied with fear and anxiety and terror. Such emotions, however reasonable, do not make for the most hoped-for bridal party pictures. Fortunately, in the end most fears were not realized. Nobody fell or was kicked in the head. The worst that happened was that everyone walked away with pictures that will bring laughter for countless years to come. From that perspective, all my reservations fade again—at least until the next creative wedding idea comes along.

STORY LESSON: I love creative wedding ideas, but more times than not they do not turn out as envisioned. Even when they do not work out, however, unless someone is seriously injured they still make good memories. As Aristotle framed it thousands of years ago, "The ideal man bears the accidents of life with dignity and grace, making the best of circumstances."[29] Nowhere do I see this played out more routinely than in wedding plans.

---

[28] The author of the quote is unknown. At least, that's what Google and Pinterest tell me.
[29] https://www.goodreads.com/quotes/7034280-the-ideal-man-bears-the-accidents-of-life-with-dignity

ONLY IN TEXAS

Some of my favorite things about Texas are barbecue, football, everything being bigger, and, of course, the rich American frontier history that has helped create modern-day America. From key commerce routes to some of the earliest farming communities and ranching depots, there is little doubt Texas played a key role in shaping our country. Ultimately, however, it was the hard-working cowboys and cowgirls who labored and protected those key economic areas that made the difference. The brave and dedicated men and women committed not only to their own survival, but also to the literal survival of others. As the demands of the job grew, traveling long miles on horseback, depending on the land for food while combating the same land for survival, so did the demand for better equipment and innovative technology to propel society forward. And perhaps no other invention proved more instrumental to doing that than the cowboy boot.

The cowboy boot's pointed tip made for easier entrance into a stirrup, locking in place when its thick protruding elevated heel engaged the foot holster, which offered solid contact and control through the toughest terrain. Knee-high leather protected its owner from thorns, barbed wire, snakes, and countless other hazards, and its elongated loops at the top were wide enough to allow for quick removal should the cowboy get hung up. Like every pivotal invention, it was born out of necessity in an effort to solve real world problems.

Dying the leather pink, embroidering fancy patterns, and inlaying corral crosses, on the other hand, was born out of fashion or boredom, I couldn't say for certain which. Not even the wildest of early cowgirls' imaginations could have envisioned this functional lifesaver as a product proudly worn during fluffy bridal pictures and in some cases to the wedding itself.

It doesn't make my list of favorite things, but it is something that I've only seen in Texas.

STORY LESSON: It's one thing to wear cowboy boots with formal attire because it's all you have; it's something entirely different when you choose it because you like them. Of course, no known clear-cut set of rules exists saying you can't wear them, but when I consider their purpose, their function, the reason for which cowboy boots exist at all, it's just difficult for me to concede that a footwear which was invented to aid the hard-working roughneck cowboys of the American frontier is the best choice for honoring a holy union between two souls. Then again, I suppose, if such a place existed for which it were, that would be Texas.

PROUD TO BE AN AMERICAN

My absolutely favorite wedding pictures involve couples with intimate ties to the military, typically as service men and women. This is partly because of my own time serving in the Army, but it also serves as a humbling reminder of all the brave soldiers who have for centuries sacrificed so much for America, the place which has afforded me more freedom than I can even appreciate.

Remembering our service men and women is easier for those of us who served during a time when double-digit percentages of Americans did, but even we often take for granted the liberties our military force affords us. The current population among whom, "for nearly two generations, no American has been obligated to join up, and few do" seem not to understand the crucial role the military plays in our democracy.[30] I wish I could say they have forgotten, but the truth is they haven't needed to know. I would argue that is all the more reason to be thankful. That our younger generation collectively has not had to lose nearly as many friends and family as the generations before is a credit to all of those former generations. And so while I'm tempted at times to get frustrated with "kids" these days who have no real compassion or empathy or honor for those serving in the military, who do not pause for even a minute on Veterans or Memorial Day to truly be thankful, what this categorically less-grateful generation has done for me, instead, is deepen the gratitude for what our soldiers have done and still do.

So each time I look through my lens with tear-filled eyes and see a group in their dress uniforms, often spanning generations, sometimes with intentionally empty spaces honoring the fallen, I humbly sing under my breath Lee Greenwood's famous chorus in "I'm Proud to be an American." Because I very much am.

STORY LESSON: This story is dedicated to all our service men and women as well as their families and friends. We have lost so many over the years and will inevitably lose many more, and I truly am grateful for what they do and have done. From the depths of my heart, thank you.

---

[30] Direct quote from Karl W. and David M. Kennedy in their *New York Times* article "Americans and Their Military, Drifting Apart," published May 26, 2013.

PAINTED SLEEVES

While tattoos have been around for literally thousands of years,[31] they have only recently made their way as a featured element on the big day. From my experience the majority of brides still want to hide their tattoo on their wedding day, but the gap is narrowing. More and more brides are featuring their ink, proudly showing off their artwork, and often incorporating the color scheme of elaborate tattoos into the day.

My favorite was the bride who incorporated the dark orange and bright pink from her tattoo sleeves into the bridesmaid dresses and flowers.[32] Like many tattoo wearers, each artwork possesses a back-story and, at least in her case, the colors did, too. The femininity of pink grounded her as a woman and, having had a mother who survived breast cancer, she'd loved the awareness it had come to represent. To honor her mom and all who have battled cancer, half her maidens wore blush dresses and half the bouquet consisted of perfectly pink peonies, coral garden roses, and flush amaryllis, bringing the small pink flowers on her right arm into reality.

---

[31] About as long a gum chewing, but not quite as long as weddings.

[32] A 'Tattoo Sleeve' is a term used to describe a large tattoo, or collection of smaller ones, that typically extend from a person's shoulder to wrist, the area that a traditional 'sleeve' would cover.

Having been diagnosed with relapsing remitting multiple sclerosis several years before, she'd also come to love the color orange, the official color of the National MS Society. Painted in various elements on her left arm, it now served as a visible reminder of daily gratitude for health. To honor her and the 2.5 million MS patients in the world, the other half of her maidens were adorned in varying muted shades of the energizing color and rounded out the floral arrangement with cantaloupe-colored dahlias, tangerine tulips, and bittersweet daisies.

The men, of course, also color coordinated their tuxedo accents with various oranges and pinks, and I remember an enviable uniqueness, a third dimension if you will, when they stood in unison and the colors literally flowed not around but through the bride, up one arm and down the other, reaching inside and embracing not only their friend but her passionate spirit.

I'll admit it: when I first noticed the tattoo trend pervade social ceremony I thought it demeaned something otherwise noble. I thought it weighted down something meant to fly. Taking pictures of this thoughtful bride, however, with her supporting entourage that communicated prosperity and hope in this new and energizing way, I realized the only thing weighted down was me.

STORY LESSON: There are certain parts of wedding tradition and social ceremony in general which I certainly hope do not ever change.[33] Cultural trends which carve themselves into society, however, will inevitably nudge their way into ceremony. This difference may be subtle—and some will be premature—but a willingness to embrace them will go a long way in not only how people perceive you, but more importantly, how you perceive yourself.

---

[33] Read the title chapter for an example.

Accidents Happen, Unfortunately[34]

Fortunately, the best man arrived for pre-ceremony pictures. Unfortunately, he was running late.

Fortunately, he was able to run. Unfortunately, he ran too fast, tripped, and fell.

Fortunately, he did not smash his face into century old wooden pews. Unfortunately, he did smash it into the floor.

Fortunately, he did not break his nose. Unfortunately, he did dislodge a front tooth.

Fortunately, someone knew a nearby dentist. Unfortunately, the dentist wasn't available.

Fortunately, the dentist would be available later. Unfortunately, later was after wedding pictures.

Fortunately, it wasn't the groom.

STORY LESSON: Accidents happen. Any reasonable human understands that; still, when you fall and lose a tooth at any time, let alone minutes before pictures at your best friend's wedding, it's difficult to accept. Such is the way with virtually every unfortunate situation, but remembering that virtually any unfortunate situation could happen to any one of us at any time goes a long way towards getting through them and an even longer way to empathy.[35]

---

[34] This chapter is inspired directly by Remy Charlip's wonderful children's book, *Fortunately*.

[35] I didn't mean for that to sound so much like a fortune cookie; but, to be fair, I might have actually read it in one.

The Throne Room

There is at least one family in south Texas who took the urban euphemism "throne room" to heart and went all out in designing their bathroom.[36] From a custom glass walk-in shower that Hollywood love scenes could have been filmed in to ornate tile work fit for Rome to custom cabinets made out of wood imported from Neverland, if there was a better or more well-thought-out room in any home anywhere that stacked up against the one I once took bridal portraits in, I cannot imagine its existence.[37] I vividly remember thinking what a peculiar answer they had given to the question, "Where are we taking the bridal portraits?" then, after experiencing the bathroom firsthand, I started developing a business plan to rent it from them!

That plan, however, never took off because, no matter how extravagant it was, the location was still a bathroom, and no amount of marketing copy could dance around that inglorious fact without flat-out lying. My only hope was to get the room formally classified as an actual throne room with the county. When I asked the owners about seeking the formal change, it turns out they had already tried. But because they were not "monarchs that presided over anything official," the county rejected the alteration!

It surprised me that the county had a formal reason, or, for that matter, that such a request could be legally denied. It did not surprise me that they had already asked.

STORY LESSON: You never know what a client is going to request or, in this case, where they are going to request it, but they have a better idea of what they want than I do (although, occasionally, my idea is better). Respect their opinion and be willing to try something that you think—or maybe even know—won't work because in the end we are wise to remember that like most things, it isn't about us anyway. And every now and then you get a really good surprise.

---

[36] Example, "I'm got to visit the throne room for awhile. Possibly a long while."

[37] For posterity, the part about the custom-made cabinets from Neverland wood is not entirely true. I am assuming the cabinets were custom made.

Syncope

Syncope (pronounced SIN-ko-pee) is the medical word for fainting, the present participle of the verb which describes experiencing a "brief loss of consciousness and posture caused by decreased blood flow to the brain."[38] A surprisingly common problem, it accounts for 3% of emergency room visits. I'd say it only occurs in 1% of weddings, although usually not to the bride or groom. It tends to happen to an unassuming bridesmaid or an over-confident groomsman. And sometimes it happens to both.

Which, I suppose, shouldn't come as a surprise. If ever there were an event that combined several key ingredients to syncope induction in continuous activity, it would be wedding ceremonies. Virtually anyone close to the ceremony will experience lots of standing around, undereating, overheating, dehydration, and, of course, stress. Add to that list any combination of unmonitored alcohol consumption, interpersonal relationship drama, unpredictable emotion swings, sprinting, jumping, unbearably boring directions and instructions, heavy lifting, long-winded preaching, unprepared and rambling speeches, never-ending dollar dances, and "other duties as required," and it certainly seems like virtually every wedding should have a syncope episode or two.

In fact, I'm pretty sure the bridesmaid and groomsman who fainted during wedding pictures within minutes of each other were batting at least .650.[39] An enviably high statistic for almost any baseball or cricket player, but when that stat line leads to a public collapse risking serious injury on a pretty significant day for someone you love, perhaps, in the game of weddings, a lower batting average is better.

STORY LESSON: So many fainting episodes are traced back to not eating enough food or drinking enough water. The simplest and most effective way to prevent syncope is to ensure everyone is properly hydrated and well fed throughout the day. All of the other "duties as required" are typically out of anyone's planning hands.

---

[38] http://www.webmd.com/brain/understanding-fainting-basics

[39] In baseball a batting average is determined by the number of hits divided by the number of at bats. So a batter who hits 1 ball every 2 times at bat is said to be batting .500 (pronounced "500 hundred"). In this case, I am suggesting the syncope mates were active in roughly 65% of the aforementioned activities.

SOUTH TEXAS SUMMER CAKE

A traditional wedding cake is comprised of three layers: a 12-inch base, a 9-inch middle, and a 6-inch top. Each layer itself consists of three sub-layers and each main section could be a different flavor, creating a practically infinite flavor combination surprise for the guests. Perhaps a trinity of red velvet, vanilla, and chocolate or maybe a triad of white chocolate raspberry, pink champagne, and carrot, the big reveal is always hidden under an incredibly artistic and intricate edible exterior that often requires an entirely separate set of people with a separate set of skills. From inspirationally themed masterpieces to elegant white chocolate pearls and lemon flavored lace, the entire wedding cake creation process requires a surprising amount of knowledge, specific tools, refrigeration space, attention to detail, people, vehicles, packing materials, ingredients, experience, and time—possibly days.

If you leave it outside in a south Texas summer, however, the sun can destroy the masterpiece in under an hour.

I don't remember whose idea it was to bring the cake outside for pre-ceremony pictures, but I can't seem to forget the horrified look on the wedding planner's face when she realized it was never brought back in. She was in mid-sentence instructing me on where to go after the ceremony, when with an unquantifiable ratio of terror, dread, and disgust, she turned and sprinted outside. I followed as fast as I could, and sure enough in place of the trifecta vanilla, red velvet, and carrot cake laid a mushy puddle of mixed-color gooey sugar bread. It was a travesty of immense proportions, a true and depressing shame. Not only because arguably the most time-intensive and central item to the celebration was utterly destroyed, but, more personally, because carrot has always been my favorite.

STORY LESSON: If the wedding cake is already staged on the table, leave it alone. Even if it's not, leave it alone. In fact, even if you know the cake maker was paid to make two of them and the backup is sitting eagerly in a cooler just waiting for some crazy accident to happen, leave…it…alone. The wedding cake is one of those rare items that has the power to overshadow just about anything else when it gets messed up. A husband could write and perform a song for the bride, the bridal party could re-enact "You're the One That I Want" from *Grease* at the reception, and the newlyweds could depart in a 1964 GTO with Jeff Gordon as the driver and all anyone will talk about later is the terrible cake story.[40]

Leave. It. Alone.

---

[40] Ok, ok…in all honesty, the 1964 GTO would make a good deal of water cooler talk the next day, with or without Mr. Gordon.

Take Two

It was one of the most memorable weddings I'd ever done. Partly because it was super fancy and partly because it was hosted by one of the wealthiest family in San Antonio, but mostly because it was the first time the shutter broke on my camera during a job. While still an issue with modern-day fancy digital cameras, when I was using their large format 2 ¼-inch ancestors, it was a catastrophe.

The shutter, simply put, controls light exposure to the sensor, creating an image based on what is visible while it's open; not terribly unlike playing peek-a-boo. Put your hands over your face, you see nothing. Opening them up, and you see a beautiful laughing baby. The image captured lives in the moment between. Keep your hands closed all the time, like the busted position mine was stuck in, and you aren't playing peek-a-boo anymore—you are playing guess-who-is-holding-an-expensive-paper-weight. Peek-a-boo is only fun when you open and close your hands; photography only works with an operating shutter.

No shutter meant no pictures. No pictures meant no job. No job not only meant no paycheck, but more importantly, it meant an unhappy client. And not just any unhappy client, but one who arguably knew more people in San Antonio and the surrounding area than anyone! A client who, if happy with my work, could open the door to countless new opportunities, but who, if unhappy, might board up every window I couldn't see.

Those heart-sinking moments are hard to forget.

But so are the overly proud ones when your forward thinking pays off. You see, I always carried around two cameras!

STORY LESSON: Budget constrains redundancy, but when your entire livelihood depends on having your tools work, you better find budget for working tools. Buying a second camera was one of the first investments I made. I think any serious photographer should do the same.

THE RECEPTION

Everyone Loves to Dance

Singer and songwriter Derek Webb tells a humorous story behind his song "Dance" in which his 90-year-old grandmother turned down a wedding proposal because the man couldn't dance.

"*She* [his grandmother] *told us* [on the phone] *to our great surprise… that this guy, her boyfriend, had gotten the nerve up and he had proposed to her,*" Webb recalls, "*but before that even sank in… she came right back and told us, 'but I just flat turned him down.'*"

"*Well, Granny, he seemed like a pretty sweet guy. How come you turned him down?*"

"*Oh, well, because he didn't know how to dance!*"[41]

There is something unique about music and dancing that stirs the soul of almost everyone. Look down at the feet of even the toughest guy, and you'll likely find toe tapping when a funky groove comes on. Look in on a mother rocking her baby to sleep and you'll not only hear her singing a song, but swaying back and forth with her newborn. Look for the bride and groom during the reception, and you'll likely find them on the dance floor alongside everyone else.

Or, rather, that's where you used to find people. Over the years fewer and fewer folks are getting up and, to paraphrase 70s disco band Peaches and Herb, "shaking their groove thing." Which is a shame because there was a time when dancing was as much a part of social convention as texting is today. A time when personal interaction and quality time together mattered more than 160-character catch phrases or three-dimensional movies. A time when even couples who married in their 90s were unwilling to have a ceremony they couldn't celebrate with two-steps and twirls.

Perhaps I'm just overly nostalgic, but I think I'm not alone when I say those days are missed.

---

[41] https://en.wikipedia.org/wiki/The_House_Show

STORY LESSON: Author William W. Purkey famously wrote that we should all strive to "Dance like there's nobody watching, love like you'll never be hurt, sing like there's nobody listening, and live like it's heaven on earth."[42] That has always felt like a pretty solid definition of what Jesus called an abundant life, but it's one that we rarely find. Regardless, to do even that first one—to dance like nobody is watching—would mean we'd have to, first, dance.

[42] https://www.goodreads.com/quotes/10123-you-ve-gotta-dance-like-there-s-nobody-watching-love-like-you-ll

A RING LOST. A RING FOUND.

Words alone would not do justice in describing the bride's expression when she realized her two-hour-old gorgeous wedding ring was no longer on her finger. The best I can do is mention that I had never witnessed anything like it before and have never seen anything like it since. If I absolutely had to choose a word, just one word, to try and describe the moment it might be "dread." Not just because the object was missing, but because in the terrifying realization the ring was gone was the even more terrifying reality it would be nearly impossible to find in their chosen outdoor spring wedding venue.

Nevertheless, within moments of the discovery, virtually the entire wedding was crawling around on hands and knees searching for the missing treasure, damaging rentals with grass stains and creating permanent memories in bridal gowns. Eventually, to everyone's surprise and relief, they found the ring! Or rather, a ring was found. It wasn't her ring that was discovered, but some other bride's wedding ring!

They spent the rest of the night and several other days searching and hoping theirs would turn up; to the best of my knowledge, it never did. They were, however, able to return the one they found to its rightful owner. That joyful experience, as only an act of great benevolence can do, helped a good deal to assuage the sorrow and frustration that lingered from their own day, although it did not erase all their own pain and frustration. The only thing that helps with something like that is hope which, to a certain degree, returning that other ring offered. After all, if they found someone else's ring, perhaps someday someone would find theirs.

STORY LESSON: I have no doubt the couple would trade that hope for not having lost their ring in the first place, but the big point here is really pretty simple: make sure the wedding rings are sized properly. In other words, make sure the darn things fit! It's easy to overlook the importance of this in favor of a big reveal and, while it's certainly rare for the ring to actually fall off, let alone become indefinitely lost, I cannot count the number of pictures I've taken where one or both of the newlyweds are either fidgeting with the too-large ring or covering up a left hand because it was too small to wear. Don't risk blemishing the day by taking this detail for granted. Trust me when I say there are plenty of other and better ways to discover hope in life than misplacing an extremely valuable and symbolic piece of jewelry.

THEY ATE A BUG

I have heard it said that the word euphemism is a euphemism for lying. I suppose that's more or less true, but the technical definition is "*a mild or indirect word or expression substituted for one considered to be too harsh or blunt when referring to something unpleasant or embarrassing.*"[43] For example, enjoying a "whole-grain sugar-free donut" is actually eating a bagel and receiving a "fast-driving award" is what you can say when you get a speeding ticket. The funniest I've heard, though, was from the mouth of a five-year-old girl who proudly announced that the rambunctious men who were now quietly absent from the reception must have eaten a bug.

The event took place in a Texas border town wedding where the father of the bride owned the ranch where the reception was located and employed his on-site ranch staff to assist with catering. Over the course of the evening, some of the staff unprofessionally fell into inebriation and created a commotion pushing and shoving each other, causing quite a distraction. Eventually, the father had no choice but to escort then men back to the house and return without them. Upon the father's return, the innocent child noted the men must have eaten a bug.

_____

[43] http://www.dictionary.com/browse/euphemism

"What's that?" I quizzed, unable to decipher the riddle.

"Those men. They ate bug."

"Why would you say that, Sweetie?"

"Because that's what Pappy says happens every time he comes back alone."

"Alone? Your grandfather escorted other men back to the house tonight?"

"Well, no, but every time one of the farm animals acts crazy, Pappy takes them for a walk and when he comes back without them, he tells us they ate a bug."

"Ah," I replied, barely able to contain my smile, "I understand now. Yea, ok, well that makes sense."

"Well, that makes one of us. I still don't get it," mumbled the innocent child.

I don't know. Maybe euphemism really is just lying after all.

STORY LESSON: 19th-century Australian surveyor and administrator Edward Counsel once wrote, "Innocence tinctures all things with the brightest hues," and there are few, if any, things more innocent than a child.[44] Try and enjoy every moment you get with your children or nieces or nephews or students because as clichéd as it is, the time really will be gone before you know it.

---

[44] http://www.notable-quotes.com/c/counsel_edward_ii.html

COME FLY WITH ME

There is a particular and noticeable energy difference when a live band performs at an event compared to the streaming of pre-recorded music. Think about how you feel experiencing the national anthem performed by an artist versus listening to a pre-recorded version digitally broadcast over the loud speaker. Even if the singer is terrible, something about the live performance ushers in a universally appreciated and arguably better atmosphere. Or consider experiencing a vibrant pianist or seasoned cellist musically escort the bride down the aisle with Pachelbel's "Canon in D" versus listening to an audio file streaming the same song but through an iPhone. There is a big difference. The most substantial difference, however, is that the former offers connectedness with humanity, inviting musicians to engage in the ceremony the same way every one else gets to—in celebration.

And celebration is, after all, what social events are about. Celebrating major events throughout history and celebrating hope for future ones. Celebrating people and that they and we matter. In my experience, musicians have a particularly interesting role because their participation in the ceremony seems to create the invisible space in which the celebration occurs. Music taps into otherwise unreachable senses and layers in a mood that can elevate the day, lifting everyone in attendance with it. This ability is, of course, inherent to music with or without live musicians. But music raises the ceiling under which the party is contained and adds depth which everyone in attendance will remember.

Ok, ok, admittedly, that last bit may be a bit over-emphasized. The bottom line is, however, that anyone can open up his or her phone and download a digital version of Frank Sinatra's "Come Fly With Me," but no one can download Frank.

STORY LESSON: Weddings, in general, are just as commonplace as music and, while I am ill equipped to say what separates great music from good, the majority of great social ceremonies I have participated in featured live music. In a time when technology has substantially lowered the cost of reproducing quality sound, an event that places an experienced musical performance as a cornerstone element really stands out. Obviously, finding the balance between elegance and affordability is something each family must figure out, but, if you manage to book a band, your event takes a substantial waltz-step closer to separating itself from the rest. And intensifying the memory of it.

CONFLICT RESOLUTION

We have all been there: replaying the argument in our mind, silently mouthing all the things we could have said, should have said, instead of the things we actually did say. All the clever comebacks run through the imagination clothed with a thick history of wrongs and pent-up frustration. Pacing back and forth, fuming with justified anger, you are one comeback away from barging back out and digging up the hatchet. We've been there with friends and lovers, but the worst is when you get there with your parents…on your wedding day.

Frustrating as that sounds, it is surprisingly common because parents tend to be unnecessarily demanding on their children during a wedding. For one, they typically fund the bulk of the event and thereby feel entitled to the majority vote on…well, everything. But parents also tend to hold onto a tradition that is fading or shifting in a different direction than they like or at least than they'd like for their children. And so like the majority of people watching those they love drift away, they get perhaps a little fearful and try to regain control. Equally human, the children fight to keep it, and that conflict often sets up a scene in which a bride might find herself increasingly upset at her mom for meddling.

I remember watching such a bride pacing in the dressing room after the ceremony, moments before the reception, her lips silently replaying the things she should have said, upset about something her mother did earlier. I could see her building up the courage to take some kind of action, readying herself to unsheathe the hatchet. I'd witnessed similar scenes a dozen times and braced for the worst. But then, in a flash, this particular bride's demeanor went from anger to resolve. Her expression somehow shifted from understandable wrath to predictable pleasure. A smile crept across her face as the light bulb in her mind permeated its way into the world. And then, in another flash, the idea took off — right with the bride and groom! Literally gone! Do not pass go, do not collect $200, and do not attend your own reception. The bride's idea was to ignore the hatchet entirely and get a head start on the honeymoon.

Apparently doing battle was just too much work. Looking back on it, I think she was right.

STORY LESSON: When you stack up the seemingly never-ending costs against the almost never-ending line of tasks associated with planning a big event, it's only a matter of time before the accumulating stress topples the pieces onto the table of relationships. While unfortunate, it's a statistical possibility. The best we can hope for is that the damage is not irreparable. While some relationships may not be worth the battle, I wouldn't offer up abandoning the remainder of the event as my first solution. For the most part, relationships, especially family ones, are worth fighting for. They are relationships worth saving. Having said that, in the above case, the great escape might still have been the best solution!

Force Majeure

Any reputable outdoor wedding venue will have a dependable plan should the weather not cooperate. For example, should a storm be expected or arrive, they might move the tables and chairs to a large outdoor covered area or building, perhaps an updated vintage barn or classic quonset, with little to no impact on the guests—the goal, after all. The thinking is quite simple and obvious: do whatever you can to ensure the guests have a good time. The plan is rooted in the timeless cliché, "Plan for the worst and hope for the best."

The majority of weather-related events are predictable. You generally have some lead time from which to enact the documented plan before hail pummels the guests. Even if the weather comes in faster than expected, the guests themselves can see the sky and take cover.

On the other hand, a newly installed water sprinkler system going off while everyone is eating gives virtually no warning at all. The pipes pressurize before anyone can identify the sound and the sprinkler heads respond, creating overlapping water arches which rapidly douse everyone and everything in a perfectly concentric path. It'll end up really funny or really upsetting. No venue has a plan for that. It's the kind of thing you learn as you go.

Welcome to marriage.

Welcome to life.

STORY LESSON: You can't control everything. This is why most contracts have a force majeure clause, to protect against "an occurrence beyond reasonable control of the venue." Whether an interrupting water sprinkler is actually force majeure is of little consequence to the bigger framing that there is no way to guarantee something unexpected will not happen on any day at any time to virtually anyone. That may well be a fine definition for life. The lesson we all have to learn is that while you cannot control everything you can take the reins on how you respond.

Spruce Cake Surprise

By definition a surprise is "an unexpected or astonishing event, fact, or thing."[45] The word exists, of course, because there are wholly expected events, facts, and things that do exist. At a wedding, for example, you expect a couple to get married, the bride to wear a beautiful wedding dress, the groom to adorn a tuxedo, and for there to be a reception. At the reception you expect there to be music, friends and family, food and drinks, and of course, cake. Sweet, tasty, delectable, extravagant, and expensive cake. Cake so moist that cutting into it would hardly be felt and for which many people come. We expect the newly married couple to start the cake-cutting ceremony by eventually making their way to that light and fluffy centerpiece, holding a lengthy knife together, smiling for pictures while laughing merrily as they revel in the moment, and then gently slice into it, successfully symbolizing their first official act together as husband and wife, showcasing to all who have joined them that they can work successfully together as a team. It's an easy first task with an easy and expected outcome—cake for all.

Unless, of course, the cake is made out of wood. Unless, of course, the cake shop delivered a demonstration-only piece that while stunning on the outside was spruce pine underneath. Even with two highly motivated people and hundreds of on-lookers rooting for you, that cake is nearly impossible to cut through and, obviously, not the kind the guests would care to eat anyway.[46]

What that kind of cake is, however, by definition is surprising.

STORY LESSON: Surely it's unnecessary to add "Be sure the wedding cake is edible" to a wedding planning checklist, but a common practice is to serve a same-tasting sheet cake to all the guests and reserve the finely decorated centerpiece for the bride and groom. While this would not wholly mitigate an impossible-to-cut doppelganger cake from showing up, it does build in a level of cake redundancy should you land in the unfortunate fraction-of-a-percent-possibility of people who end up with an inedible primary one.

---

[45] http://www.dictionary.com/browse/surprise

[46] At least, with a wedding knife anyway. An 18V-reciprocating saw would do the trick, but, honestly, how many weddings have readily available power tools?

Go Roman!

People offer encouragement and support in lots of ways. For example, giving gifts. Lots of folks spend a good deal of their hard-earned money on other people to show they care for them, to support their life efforts in some tangible and practical way. Regrettably, sometimes those gifts come tied to an expectation, but rarely is that the case when honoring someone in social ceremony. Indeed, despite vast and jaded skepticism, a good deal of gift-giving stems from unfiltered love.

Another, less costly way to show one you appreciate them is words of affirmation. Whether conveyed through a hand-written letter or a stock card or a performed song, the main objective is similar to the giving of gifts—to show the receiving parties that they matter. This public or private display is often considered more valuable than a physical purchase because it requires thought, creativity, and even sometimes carries risk. Like the time a group of seven groomsmen, after toasting the groom, simultaneously turned around to proudly reveal "GO ROMAN" across their collective backs, publicly displaying their support for the man of the hour. Lots of things could have gone wrong: a letter falling off, the twisting of an ankle, or position N missing the cue and only displaying "GO ROMA" in an awkward display of tomato affection. None of that happened, thankfully. The timing was perfect and, in the end, the risk was worth the reward because not only was it funny, but everyone understood that putting together a gift like that meant they had to spend something they can never get back—time.

And, of course, fortunately, for them, RAMON understood that. Or he might have wished they had invested just a few more seconds and swapped the positional O for the positional A and spelled his name correctly!

STORY LESSON: Generally speaking, all bets are off when alcohol is involved, but the above error could have easily been avoided. Still, if this is the worst unplanned event at your wedding, then you fall into the highest percentage of the fortunate. Roll with life's punches and, when possible, marry someone with a reasonably good sense of humor. It'll save you from more situations than you can possibly imagine.

Monkey Business

Wedding etiquette for divorced parents can be tricky, especially when it comes to the place where all key contributors of the day will be in closest proximity—the receiving line. While not required, a receiving line marks the best opportunity to ensure the welcoming and thanking of every guest, which is good etiquette for any size party. Tradition holds the hosts of the event (typically the bride's parents, mother then father) welcome first, followed by the other set of parents, and eventually ending with the bride and groom. In the case of the divorced, however, people have to get creative, because quite often, "Divorce is not as much about failing at marriage as it is winning at bitterness and resentment," neither of which is a welcoming sentiment anyone wants their guests to experience.[47]

This depressing truth teaches that it's often safer to keep divorced parents apart as best you can, rather than ask them to put their emotions aside for even half an hour.[48] And in the most extreme circumstances, it might mean not inviting one of them or, perhaps, just replacing Dad with a monkey. Indeed, sometimes the bitterness valley runs so deep that standing in the traditional place of Dad might be a capuchin monkey, which according to his ex-wife, the mother of the bride, "is not only cuter and more friendly, but smarter, too."

I can't say for certain, of course, as I never met the man, but anyone who has ever seen a capuchin monkey, like the ones famously used in *Pirates of the Caribbean, Dr. Doolittle,* and *Night at the Museum*, might be inclined to agree.

STORY LESSON: Especially in the case of bitter divorcees, clearly communicating expectations is key to a successful day. From my experience, virtually all adults can put aside their differences for one day to celebrate the life of someone they love, but when one or both of them are surprised things can unravel. Every situation is different but, like so many of life's problems, if we just talked to each other a little more, maybe we'd find some solutions.

---

[47] A loose paraphrase of an unknown divorce quote that goes, "Try not to think of divorce as failing at marriage but rather winning at bitterness and resentment."

[48] Which is arguably even more depressing.

To Strapless or Not To Strapless

For a multitude of reasons dresses with straps have lost favor over the years. Whether keeping up with contemporary style, trying to balance out material design, or simply a desire to show more shoulder, the modern-day image of the bride and her troupe almost exclusively feature women in strapless dresses. For all the fashion upsides they possess, however, one considerable downside is the inability to ensure that the dress remains in place. The basic and most fundamental design principle of a dress with straps virtually guarantees the top won't fall down bearing who-knows-what for all to see. Indeed, if I had a nickel for every bride or bridesmaid that came out of her top at some point during the celebration, I'd have been able to retire years ago!

For the most part, it happens on the dance floor 30 seconds into some call-to-action song like Van Halen's "Jump," but the most interesting is when it happens in the fight for the flowers during the bouquet toss. Women go to acrobatic lengths to secure the supposed prize for imminent marital fortune. When you combine an aggressive disposition with an inadequately altered outfit with little to no support, odds are good someone is going to get a show. I saw a woman once so focused on winning that she didn't even realize she had come clean out of her top until several moments after her victory. It was quite the scene. Given the number of men who came to her aid, the leap and in this case the dress may have been worth it. Admittedly I liked the dress selection, too; had she chosen one with straps, I'd have been out a nickel.

STORY LESSON: In reality, dropping the top doesn't happen too often, but it does happen. The more bothersome issue with wearing strapless dresses, however, is watching women fidgeting with their tops all day long, constantly repositioning the front. Some women are clearly more self-conscious about the potential mishap than others; either way, if you're going to go strapless, budget a little more for custom tailoring. The only thing possibly worse than having the dress actually fall off is spending the entire evening worrying about it.

JOY JUICE

The term "drunk as a sailor" stems from the alcohol consumption of Navy men once they make port after a lengthy time at sea. Since 1914 the U.S. Navy's alcohol policy has been zero tolerance, and so short of a Beer Day—a one-day authorization, which allows for beer consumption aboard the ship—every 45 days, the men aboard ship would have been sans joy juice since at least their deployment date. The combination, then, of abstinence-induced lowered tolerance and affectionate reminiscing combine to make the newly landed service man surprisingly inebriated more quickly than expected. In other words, they get piss drunk really easily.

A similar combination of circumstances exists at weddings where the celebrating couple may fast from alcohol to lose weight for the event, then typically not eat enough amidst entertaining all the guests, and are pumped up on natural adrenaline from the excitement. Add to that trio the constant toasts from extended family and random liquor shots from a seemingly infinite number of friends. That quintet often collapses on the bride and/or groom causing them actually to collapse themselves unexpectedly—like, say, during a thank-you speech.

Chalk it up to "shit happens," I suppose, but there are still few things more embarrassing than passing out from drunkenness. And passing out from drunkenness while giving your keynote speech has to be at the top of that list.

STORY LESSON: I understand how easily such inebriation can occur, but it's also easily preventable. Eat some food, turn down a shot or two, or maybe just dance a little more. Passing out on your big day is not something you want to do. When you look back on your wedding day and reflect on that moment, my guess is you will find no good reason for having gotten that drunk. Sailors, at least, served their country.

THE GETAWAY

KARMA. OR JUST BAD LUCK.

One of my favorite wedding traditions stems from the Tudor period in England when people would throw their shoes at the departing wedding carriage for good luck.[49] Of course, as many of us intuitively understand, shoe throwing can be quite dangerous. So eventually people opted to tie shoes to the bumper instead. After a predictable rise in barefoot people complaining about missing shoes, the tradition morphed into tying tin cans to the back of the car.[50]

At least that's one rendition of the tin-can history. Another tin-can tradition claims the rattling warns off evil spirits during departure. A third story claims it keeps the bride and groom from running off early by making an obnoxious racket should they try. Regardless of which story or combinations of them are true, wedding parties (typically, the

[49] http://mentalfloss.com/article/17737/3-bizarre-wedding-customs-nobody-questioned-until-now
[50] I do not have any proof that there was an actual rash of barefoot people as a result of bumper shoe tying in the 1500s or any other century for that matter.

men) tend to vandalize the exit vehicles of newlyweds; for the most part, that vandalism is benign. But every now and again it's not the newly married couple who gets hurt but the vandals.

Like the Uvalde wedding I did where one of the groomsmen decided right as the car was departing that it needed a little more shoe polish. With almost no provocation (blood alcohol level excluded), he boldly ran alongside the car illegibly scribbling, his humorous reputation linearly escalating alongside the vehicle's speed. His reputation, not to mention his physical well-being, quickly headed south when his shirtsleeve hung up on rear door handle and the vehicle began to drag him along. To this day I'm not sure if the driving groom didn't notice or just didn't like him, but eventually the fabric tore and the groomsman-turned-comedian fell to the ground alongside his pride and his sobriety.

Fortunately, he was fine. Unfortunately, none of it was caught on film. Either way the episode taught me that while throwing shoes is dangerous for the bride and groom, drinking while shoe polishing a car is dangerous for the wedding party.

STORY LESSON: When it comes to tradition, you never know who is going to "one-up" the norm, but it always carries risk. The best we can hope for is that the risk provides enough reward to make it worth the gamble and, of course, that nobody gets hurt. It's not always easy to see the humor or appreciate the effort that goes into it, but understanding that the people doing it really do have good intentions helps. It also helps when they end up (safely) in the dirt.

LEAVING ON A JET PLANE

If you ever find yourself on the airport tarmac with a newlywed couple as they board their private jet headed for Los Angeles to depart for their final honeymoon destination and they ask if you want to go with them, the answer should unequivocally be yes. There are, of course, some obvious exceptions for which the answer is no: for example, if you're expecting a baby in the next few hours, or if there is a federal injunction prohibiting your traveling via air. Otherwise, almost everyone else in the world will understand your decision to go. Aside from the markedly faster travel time, some private jets often come equipped with robust lounges, full-size bathrooms, personal chefs, and who-knows-what other customized options. Plus, experiencing a trip like this puts you in a teeny tiny class of people who can say they have done it.

When I walked in the door to my house at four in the morning from such an invitation, several long hours after my expected arrival time home, it was all my wife Betty could do not to strangle me for putting her through a night of terrible anxiety. This was before the days when everyone and their mother and their eight-year-old children had cell phones, and Betty had been imagining the worst. For all she knew I was lying dead in a ditch somewhere and she, rightfully, let me have more than an earful. Once I filled her in, once I told her I had flown in a private jet to and from Los Angeles, we fired up the coffee pot and started making breakfast, because she wanted to know every detail.

I had hoped when I said, "Yes," to the invite hours earlier that Betty would forgive me, and I remember feeling immensely relieved when she actually did. I think the forgiveness came easily because she would have made the same decision, and she knew I would have encouraged it. After all, she wasn't expecting and, as far as I knew, the federal government hadn't grounded her.

STORY LESSON: An occasional surprise (often a perk) of any services profession is a gratuity, which may come in many forms. Learning how to accept it (and not expect it) is a trade secret that I am convinced cannot be taught. It has to be individually learned through time and repetition, which inevitably means success as well as failure. I am so grateful for the seemingly countless people I have met in my career and for the many opportunities they have afforded me and those I love. For your life's work, be sure to do something you like. Or, if possible, do something that you absolutely love. It might or might not bring you fame and fortune, but it will absolutely bring you joy. Maybe even a ride on a jet plane.

HOT AIR BALLOON

No matter how much you plan, not every creative idea works out well. For example, having a bride and groom marry inside a fully inflated hot air balloon, its dominating presence and beauty metaphorically foreshadowing their life ahead, may sound really exciting on paper. When actually enacted, however, the metaphor may communicate something else entirely.

While the colorful massive ball will certainly serve as a stand-out marker for the wedding site from miles away and provides an unmatchable "wow" factor to guests, keeping the globe inflated requires air and almost exclusively hot air which will not, no matter your wishes, contain itself inside the magic bubble. Invariably the laws of physics prevail, and a good amount of heat blows back on the passengers which, while welcome at 2,000 feet above the ground traveling at the speed of wind, is most certainly not welcomed by a bride with a painted face standing still for half an hour.

Heat isn't the real problem, however. The real problem in getting married inside the basket of a hot air balloon is ensuring the globe remains grounded—at least, for as long as you want it to be. Fundamentally speaking, a hot air balloon's ability to float works principally on some fancy thermodynamic framing that hot air is less dense than cold air and, thereby, experiences a significant buoyant upward force when inflated.[51] This desire to rise, of course, can be combated with good old fashioned rope and tie downs, but predicting how a strong gust of wind will impact an 800-pound 50-foot canopy already itching to take off is damn near impossible.

The first gust that lifts the basket a few inches is kind of funny and most definitely surprising but, once the first rope comes loose and the balloon starts moving laterally, Startle and Humor quickly give way to Uncertainty and Embarrassment. Surprisingly, right about the time the sprinting pastor yells out, "You may now kiss the bride!" and the balloon takes off, the same Joy and Celebration that show up to every wedding make their way into ones like these, too.

STORY LESSON: Unless you can control the weather, I advise against gambling too much with flying entrances or exits. Some ideas really are better left to the imagination.

---

[51] This is more commonly stated as "hot air rises." Yes, of course, I could have just written that, but working in the word 'thermodynamics' into a book someday without being a scientist is on my bucket list; or, rather, it used to be.

HORSE POWER

The word *carriage* has roots in Old Northern French and translates "to carry in a vehicle."[52] The earliest and best known of these vehicles, of course, is horse drawn—e.g., the Egyptian chariot famously used to help win countless battles. Like all good innovations, its utility extended well beyond a single domain, and other cultures, like the Romans and Chinese, improved the design and created wagons used to propel civilization forward by allowing rapid transport of materials and merchandise.

Over time other amenities arrived, such as cushioned seats, hard rooftops, and privacy doors, and the modernized cart adapted a new name—the coach, which quickly cornered the traveling market. Gaining more in popularity with improved stability and steering eventually launched this ancestor of the luxury sedan into a new class called the carriage which became known for transporting the wealthiest and most prominent people around. Its long-standing run came to end as steam propulsion and other research

---

[52] https://en.wikipedia.org/wiki/Carriage

gained momentum and the demand for carriages, along with the powerful horses which pulled them, began to fade away.

I think about that rich 3500-year history every time I see a newlywed couple leave in a classic horse-drawn carriage. In particular, I think about how, despite all that change and progress, at the heart of each iteration stood the timeless and unchanging horse. It was literally horse-power that enabled the earliest chariot riders to proclaim victory, the original coach drivers to transport rocks and wood, and the most noble of lords and ladies to roam freely throughout their domain.

I think about that and then I think about how unpleasant the smell must have been. I mean, horses aren't nearly as bad as a skunk or a musk ox, but has anyone been around a horse-drawn carriage that smells good?! It never fails: every time I take pictures of a couple leaving in a horse-drawn carriage, the odor nearly knocks me out. It could just be my overly sensitive olfactory system but, with all the great minds who came up with all the wonderful innovations to the horse-drawn carriage over the last few thousand years, I wish someone had found a way to improve on that!

STORY LESSON: You never know what you're going to run into, so along with a change of clothes I also carry around a set of ear and nose plugs just in case. They cost only a few dollars, but the headache they can save you is priceless.

God's Paintbrush

When it comes to booking a wedding venue, amenities make a big difference. From easing the planning burden with all-inclusive pricing to offering bed and breakfast stays for the entire wedding party, the thinking is obvious—the more unique offerings, the more likely clients will choose that business. The most unique amenity I've seen came at a wealthy neighborhood community in San Antonio in the form of something banned in quite a few places these days: fireworks.

While primarily a residential neighborhood, its footprint in the hill country and affluent constituent base made the location a prime location for very classy weddings. And with premiere service often come creative celebration ideas. So while I can't say I was surprised when I first saw the custom fireworks display as the bride and groom departed, I can say I was more than impressed. Few symbols, if any, better communicate the internal joy and excitement people feel during a celebration than exploding lights, as the nearly indescribable color palate paints shapes on a perfect South Texas night sky.

When the final brush strokes paint the words "Congratulations" followed by the couple's names, it feels as if God himself might be holding the brush. And who is to say He isn't? After all, I've always heard Texas is God's country, right?

STORY LESSON: Just about every wedding venue is going to be amazing. Be on the lookout for what makes each one unique and try and capture that particular piece during the day. Just like the venue is doing their best to honor the bride and groom, do your best to honor them.

Don't Rock The Boat

People are drawn to San Antonio, Texas, for lots of very good reasons. Along with a reasonable cost of living, San Antonio has a deep rich American history, rarely experiences natural disasters, has virtually year-round golf, and, like Paris, there's a river running through it.

While not nearly as large as the Seine River flowing from the Alps, the San Antonio River has a benevolent history rooted in missionary work at the turn of the 17th century when the city was founded and the area named after St. Anthony de Padua, known for his undying love and devotion to the poor and the sick.[53] That original "serving others" value instilled by its earliest founders and its namesake has carried the city forward hundreds of years. Today the natural flowing centerpiece continues to "serve others" by bolstering the city's economy, continuously drawing tourism along its Riverwalk, and strengthening its urban fabric by offering a unique landscape to draw in the next generation. A fabric in which you can get married in the middle of the city and then leave in a boat!

Indeed, snapping photos of a metropolitan bride and groom departing the big city in a boat on a natural flowing spring, metaphorically marrying urban lifestyle with rustic nature, is one of my favorite leave-taking shots. Unless, of course, the over-zealous wedding party accidently rocks the boat jumping back onto land and the newlyweds fall into the water. If that happens, you quickly wish city and nature had left each other alone.

STORY LESSON: Be wary of water. This is obvious, but it can't be said enough. While lots of people have great temperaments when it comes to the unexpected, I think few will have a positive disposition towards unexpected immersion. Although I suppose if you are going to risk water, doing it at the end of the wedding, when your clothes are on the way off anyway, is as good a time as any.

---

[53] https://en.wikipedia.org/wiki/Anthony_of_Padua

Happiness and a Harley

Few wedding exits have left a bigger image in the reel of my memory than that of a fully dressed bride and groom rolling off into the sunset on brand new Harley Davidson motorcycles. The image is so vivid because newlyweds leaving on motorcycles happens so infrequently and also because the contrast between raw open-road riding and pristine outerwear is so stark, but the main reason I remember the sparkling metallic chrome scene is the way in which they unveiled the big surprise.

Having already put in several hundred miles on the roads, the couple had obtained their motorcycle licenses several months before, fallen almost as much in love with riding as with each other, and dreamed about riding off into the sunset on their wedding day. But they also wanted the exit to be a big surprise, so they had not told anyone about their new hobby. As the wedding celebration came to an end, they walked through the traditional shower of rice to a classic black limo. Then instead of pulling away, the couple exited the limo on the other side, mounted their pre-staged hogs, and fired up the 80db-trademarked V-Twin engines startling everyone within earshot! As the limo pulled away, it revealed the happy Harley couple who gave a quick wave good-bye and then, as if starring in a contemporary western, rode off into the sunset.

I have heard it said, "You can't buy happiness, but you can buy a Harley Davidson and that's kind of the same thing." Having put more than 50,000 miles on my own hog, I agree.[54]

STORY LESSON: If you can, stay until the end of the wedding. It not only represents your support for the couple, but you never know what kind of surprises you'll get to witness. Statistically, you're probably going to witness the ordinary. But just like the greatest comebacks in sports history, every now and then there will be something remarkably unexpected, and you'll get to say you were there for it.

---

[54] For posterity, I owned an FXRP, arguably the best handling Big Twin Harley ever made.

Parties are Supposed to End

Weddings are generally all-day events for the bride and groom. From being up early to getting involved with last-minute planning decisions to standing on their feet all day to countless hand-shaking to dancing with countless friends and family to lengthy leave-taking, the day somehow simultaneously flies by and takes forever. When the hours are added, it can easily round up to a full 24 for the newly married couple.

On top of that, consider that if nerves did not contribute to a poor night's rest, the wedding party may have stolen them for one last night out, so by the time the wedding comes to its planned conclusion and the moment to be alone for the first time as husband and wife finally arrives, the last thing the exhausted couple wants to discover is the entire wedding party hiding inside the limo.

"Surprise! The party's just getting started, dude!" may literally be the absolutely last thing they want to hear when they open the door to the limousine. So when the couple simultaneously responds with, "Holy shit! Get the hell out of here!" please understand it's not personal. It's just been a really long day.

STORY LESSON: No matter how good or funny an idea seems, if it delays the bride and groom's exit in any way, do not do it. We should do our very best to remember the day is all about celebrating the couple and of all the wedding activities that they want to celebrate. The one you are slowing down is the one they have been looking forward to the most.

DOWNTOWN QUARTER HORSES

Leaving on horseback in a big city presents an interesting set of challenges. First, there is the issue of permitting. While in a pre-Model-T world infrastructure existed to support horse transportation, cities have long abandoned hitching rails, and street sweepers these days have an entirely different set of expectations for their daily duty.[55] As such, laws typically exist to prevent livestock from roaming in the streets.

Assuming you can get an exception permit, however, the next obstacle is transportation and parking. Someone actually has to deliver the horses and, while most reception venues have roomy vendor delivery areas, not all are set up for unloading two or more standard 15-hand quarter horses. Conceptually, this might seem like a non-issue, but I witnessed such a scene and it may be the most daunting obstacle to overcome.

---

[55] You see what I did right there? No modern-day city street worker thinks it's their duty to clean up horse doody....☺

Then, of course, there is the attire one sports for leaving. While a tad restrictive, men can get away with wearing a standard tuxedo; horse-back riding is not a common consideration by the wedding dress design teams, however. As such, the bride will either have to change into another outfit or sneak on a pair of white riding tights. Either way, failure to do so will greatly increase the chance of lower body exposure or injury.

Which brings us to the issue of personal safety. Falling off a horse, in general, is never a good thing. But falling off a horse onto a concrete street on your wedding day may be the worst combination of "time" and "place" possible.

If you can get past all these challenges, it really is a beautiful scene. Well, at least, I imagine it is. I haven't seen anyone get past them. Yet.

STORY LESSON: As a general rule for social ceremony planning, certain risks just aren't worth taking. Sometimes our creative ideation gets the best of us but, if Sartre is right and we are our choices, choose wisely and leave in a limo.

THE DROP OFF

Although an ever-present possibility for a pilot in the aArmy, jumping out of a plane never made it onto my bucket list. Needing to record flight time to maintain my pilot certification, however, I certainly did not have a problem if people wanted to jump out of mine! So when a skydiving couple asked me if I would fly them up so they could jump out and get married and then fly them up a second time for their departure from the reception, I "jumped" at the chance to fly twice in one day.

The big question I had was who was marrying them? While I never specifically asked the ministers I had met, I was pretty sure they shared my passion for staying inside moving vehicles. Well, surprisingly, there are only two requirements to becoming an ordained officiant in the State of Texas—you have to be over the age of 18 and able to complete an online application![56] Fortunately, one of their skydiving friends met both of those requirements and, when the big day arrived, I was not only able to be an integral part of a special day for a new couple but logged a few more hours in my flight book.

Oh, and since I happened to be over the age of 18 and had a computer with internet, I went ahead and became a minister, too. That decision helped out more times than I can remember.[57]

STORY LESSON: Being knowledgeable in a wide range of disciplines is important to success. Obviously, it does not lead to success, and you can otherwise be successful, but there are so many resources available to us, especially with the invention of the internet, that not only can anyone become a renaissance man or woman, but I think they should!

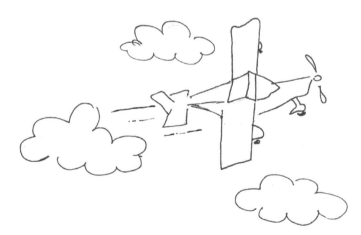

---

[56] There are, of course, lots of other ways to be ordained and I would recommend exploring those. If you're in a pinch, though, universalministries.com is where I got mine!
[57] Read "Where's the Minister"